W9-BVV-808

Twayne's United States Authors Series

EDITOR OF THIS VOLUME

Kenneth Eble

University of Utah

W. E. B. Du Bois

TUSAS 399

W. E. B. Du Bois
National Portrait Gallery, Smithsonian Institution
Washington, D.C.

W. E. B. DU BOIS

By JACK B. MOORE
University of South Florida

TWAYNE PUBLISHERS
A DIVISION OF G. K. HALL & CO., BOSTON

Wingate College Library

Copyright © 1981 by G. K. Hall & Co.

Published in 1981 by Twayne Publishers,
A Division of G. K. Hall & Co.
All Rights Reserved

Printed on permanent/durable acid-free paper and bound
in the United States of America

First Printing

Library of Congress Catologing in Publication Data

Moore, Jack B.
W. E. B. Du Bois.

(Twayne's United States authors series: TUSAS 399)
Bibliography: p. 174-81
Includes index.
1. Du Bois, W. E. B. (William Edward Burghardt),
1868-1963. 2. Afro-Americans—Biography.
I. Title. II. Series.
E185.97.D73M66   303.4'84'0924   81-2425
          ISBN 0-8057-7329-0   AACR2

088703

For Clara, my mother

Contents

About the Author

Jack B. Moore was born in Newark, New Jersey, in 1933. He received the B.A. from Drew University, the M.A. from Columbia University, and the Ph.D. from the University of North Carolina at Chapel Hill. He has taught at Fourah Bay College as a Fulbright Fellow, the University of West Virginia, Washington and Lee University, and is currently Chairman of the American Studies Department at the University of South Florida. His short stories have appeared in such periodicals as *Esquire*, *New Mexico Quarterly*, and *Kansas Quarterly* and have won prizes. He has written frequently on American, Afro-American, and African culture and literature for magazines including the *Mississippi Quarterly*, *Studies in Short Fiction*, and the *Journal of African Studies*. He has written or edited a number of books on American literature, including *Maxwell Bodenheim* (New York: Twayne, 1970). He is married to Judith B. Moore, a social worker, and they have five children.

Preface

Like the hero of Walt Whitman's epic "Song of Myself," William Edward Burghardt Du Bois contained multitudes within himself, an amazing and dazzling variety of which he let out into the world. But which among that company of talents was the essential man who harnessed all the identities that Du Bois sent forth, and what ideological cords did he employ to draw together the many attitudes this black Proteus voiced during his lifetime? How did Du Bois prevent himself—his selves—from becoming a fragmented man, a genius in pieces?

These are the basic questions the present study pursues, questions to be confronted but not necessarily answered completely, precisely because of Du Bois's complexity and the great range and sometimes evolving, shifting nature of his thinking. Although he revealed much about himself in his many published autobiographical recollections he also concealed much. Furthermore, he produced an intimidating mass of literature during his extraordinarily long and productive life—poems, plays, novels, essays, polemics, journalistic features, biographies, and academic studies. But a unity and coherence runs through his life and most of his thought, so that both can be examined with profit, especially in an age like ours when so many public thinkers seem to be either men and women of stunted, parochial interests or wide-drifting pundits blown like gaseous balloons over the surface of the latest trends.

One part of my study examines briefly the chief events and controversies of Du Bois's life, because even a brief biography of such an important public figure and writer can help satisfy our curiosity about how he attained his dual role in our culture. His life is also significant because, unlike most writers, Du Bois was in reality and not just in his private fantasies a preeminent spokesman on crucial political issues bearing upon America's racial problems. For over a quarter of a century (roughly from the time he wrote *The Souls of Black Folk* in 1903 until his first departure from the NAACP in 1934) he was an internationally recognized, major black American political figure, although because of the racial oppression he constantly attacked, his black electorate was disproportionately weak at the national level. Much of his life assumes an added significance, therefore, because of his intimate role in the history of agitation against inequality.

My main and most difficult job has been to examine Du Bois's literary achievement. I have analyzed his major works in order to introduce the reader to the central ideas of these works, to note how the ideas relate to the overall impression a particular work creates, and to indicate how the ideas of one book connect to ideas in the other books. I have based my review of his major and most seminal works upon a fair appraisal of how substantially his ideas and contentions are argued, not upon whether or not I personally agree with them.

I have also attempted to investigate the ways he presented his ideas, his verbal strategies. When Du Bois wrote he nearly always intended to teach his audience about the issues close to him. But as a didactic writer he was usually a craftsman and sometimes an artist. He sought to reproduce his ideas with clarity and persuasiveness, appropriate effects of tone and mood, beauty or harshness, to enable him to command attention from those to whom he delivered his messages. He shaped his utterances to his audiences' needs and abilities, frequently achieving startlingly good results whether he was addressing a crowd of school children or academic professionals. Sometimes he missed his rhetorical mark wildly, usually by overwriting, but he was always conscious of literary aims and of the devices a good writer must command to communicate with grace and power: one of the courses at Harvard he most revered was freshman composition.

I have sketched the unusual paths Du Bois's life took from its ordinary and low start in a small Massachusetts town shortly after the Civil War ended, to its surprising and yet logical termination in the newly created African nation of Ghana, when Du Bois was an internationally recognized and respected and, by some, hated man of the world. I have also noted his significant and hard-earned achievements along the way as a scholar, a race leader, and a writer, trying to keep always in my mind and the mind of my imagined reader, that all these multiple strands of Du Bois's life and thought form a single network whose designs, while complicated, all stem from the paradoxical character of Du Bois himself.

Preface

In a thought-provoking chapter titled "The Paradox of W. E. B. Du Bois" in his *Negro Thought in America, 1880–1915,* August Meier discussed some of the roles that made Du Bois such a formidable figure to understand: "scholar and prophet; mystic and materialist; ardent agitator for political rights . . . a Marxist who was fundamentally a middle-class intellectual." My study attempts to illustrate how Du Bois functioned in these roles and in others, how he expressed his divergent ideas, and, ultimately, how those ideas tended to reinforce the view that all of mankind must be given the best chance possible to live a good life.

Perhaps because his own being was so paradoxical he could maintain in suspension, like a juggler (a fumbling juggler sometimes), many sympathies and longings, even while containing intense hostilities and emotional twists. He was a small-town boy and he was a man of the world. He was passionate and icy, haughty, warm, and friendly, compassionate and filled with hate. He was ethnocentric and an internationalist, a pacifist (mostly) who was extremely receptive to revolution. He berated his fellow Negroes every time he felt they failed—especially in running their educational institutions—to follow the paths he had decided were the only true roads to progress, and he eloquently condemned the white world for forcing black people into patterns of failure or unfairly limited success. He spread the gospel of the mission belonging to the black, elite, "talented tenth" in the Negro's quest for independence from white oppression, while preaching the grandeur of the anonymous black masses who, uneducated and unprepared for freedom, nonetheless exhibited almost unbelievable folk wisdom and civic understanding and charity during the Reconstruction era when briefly they participated meaningfully in shaping Southern society.

He was a segregationist and an integrationist, a black activist who also emphasized the mutual interests of hostile groups such as the Southern poor whites and rural blacks who seemed to relate to each other only in bitter conflict. Arnold Rampersad in his book on Du Bois notes how inconsistent were others' views of him: Sinclair Lewis declared that his "sense of humor" was "equal to his scholarship," while Claude McKay remarked upon his "cold, acid hauteur," and James Weldon Johnson reported he was both "the most jovial and fun-loving of men" and "cold, stiff, supercilious." Within him dwelled a moralizing New England puritan with a strong sense of calling and self-discipline and a stiff personal reticence; a contentious

Victorian in his earnestness and sometimes in his stuffiness and often in his lapses into maudlin sentimentality and in his predilection for heavily embellished prose; a thoroughly modern thinker in his urgent calls for radical social change in the lives of Negroes, women, the poor—in all the impoverished lives he saw around him; and a Negro in what he would term the soul of his being.

My goal amid this jumble of paradoxes and the rich variety of ways that Du Bois behaved and thought and wrote, is to present the basic facts and configurations of his life along with a critical examination of his chief ideas and the literary works which best present them. In this manner I hope to enable the reader to understand better both Du Bois and the literature he produced. I believe the reader will come to see a unity in both, but a complex unity with room inside it for some understandable contradictions.

In this study I have focused mainly upon Du Bois rather than upon his critics; consequently I have avoided detailed discussion of the controversial reception of many of Du Bois's ideas. I have noted a few of the more important conflicts he engaged in, such as his notorious controversy with Booker T. Washington, but I have not examined each and every instance of debate that others had with him.

I have tended to use the terms Negro, colored, black, and Afro-American in a manner appropriate to what I was discussing, following the lead of my sources and, for example, using the term "colored" when Du Bois did. I also followed my own taste which I hope is sensitive and understanding if not always conversant with the very latest fashion. In an attempt to minimize obtrusive and excessive documentation, which can be especially annoying in a work such as this—which is intended for a general audience and written about a writer most of whose books are not yet available in a standard, scholarly edition—I have usually footnoted only when I felt the reader could not locate my source by using common sense.

I would like to thank International Publishers for permission to quote material from *The Autobiography of W. E. B. Du Bois*, © 1968, the University of Massachusetts Press for permission to quote from Volumes 1 and 2 of *The Correspondence of W. E. B. Du Bois*, edited by Herbert Aptheker, © 1973-1978, and Mr. David Du Bois for permission to quote extracts from *Black Reconstruction in America*, © 1935, and *Dusk of Dawn*, © 1940.

University of South Florida   JACK B. MOORE

Chronology

1868   William Edward Burghardt Du Bois born 26 February in Great Barrington, Massachusetts.

1883–   Correspondent for the *New York Age, New York Globe,*
1885   and other black newspapers.

1884   June, graduates from Great Barrington High School; gives Valedictory speech on Wendell Phillips. Mother Mary dies in the autumn. Works for a year at odd jobs.

1885–   Attends Fisk University, entering as a sophomore. Works
1888   summers in schools around Nashville. Receives B.A. in 1888; speaks at graduation on Bismark.

1888   Enters Harvard University as a junior.

1890   Receives B.A. (*cum laude*) in philosophy; gives commencement speech on Jefferson Davis. Enters graduate study in history.

1891   Receives M.A. in history from Harvard. Begins study for the doctorate.

1892   Receives grant (half gift, half loan) from Slater Fund enabling him to study in Europe. Attends University of Berlin; travels for two years in Western Europe.

1894   Returns to U.S. in the summer, riding steerage. August, accepts position as chairman of Classics Department at Wilberforce University.

1895   Receives Ph.D. in history from Harvard, commends Booker T. Washington for his September 18 Atlanta Exposition speech.

1896   Marries Nina Gomer. *Suppression of the African Slave-Trade* published. Leaves Wilberforce; accepts fifteen-month appointment to do field work in Philadelphia's Seventh Ward.

1897   Accepts position at Atlanta University. Edits *Atlanta University Studies.*

1899   Sam Hose lynched. *The Philadelphia Negro.*

1900   July, attends first Pan-African Congress, in London; elected secretary. Attends Paris Exposition.

1903   Anti-Washington "Boston Riots" during which Monroe Trotter is jailed. Du Bois defends Trotter. *The Souls of Black Folk.*

1905   Niagara Movement organized; holds first conference in Fort Erie, Ontario.

1906   Founds periodical *The Moon* (which lasts one year). Atlanta pogrom. August, organizes second Niagara Conference at Harper's Ferry.

1907   Third Niagara Conference, in Boston. Founds *Horizon,* published until 1910.

1908   Niagara movement in decline. Fourth Conference in Oberlin, Ohio.

1909   Last Niagara Conference, at Sea Isle, New Jersey. National Negro Committee meets (what will become the National Association for the Advancement of Colored People) with Du Bois attending. *John Brown.*

1910   Accepts offer to become director of publications and research for NAACP. Summer, leaves Atlanta and arrives in New York. November, edits first issue of *The Crisis,* official publication of the NAACP.

1911   July, attends Universal Races Conference in London. *The Quest of the Silver Fleece.*

1913   Pageant "The Star of Ethiopia" presented successfully in New York and Washington.

1915   Booker T. Washington dies. *The Negro.*

1916   First Amenia Conference held at home of Joel Spingarn.

1918   Famous "Close Ranks" editorial in *The Crisis* advocating Negro participation in World War I. December, Du Bois sails for Europe to investigate condition of black troops.

1919   Infamous "Red Summer" in America, with numerous attacks upon black citizens. *The Crisis* has over 100,000 subscribers. Du Bois organizes Pan-African Congress in Paris (called by some the "first," and by others the "second" Conference).

1920   Founds, edits *Brownies Book* for children. *Darkwater.* Controversy with Marcus Garvey begins.

1921   Pan-African Congress in London, Brussels, and Paris.

1923   Receives Spingarn Medal. Organizes Pan-African Congress in London, Paris, and Lisbon. Represents U.S.A. at inauguration of president of Liberia. Attacks Garvey in February issue of *The Crisis.*

1924   *The Gift of Black Folk.*
1926   Spends two months in Soviet Russia. Founds Krigwa Players, black repertory theater group in Harlem.
1927   Krigwa Players win little theater award, in New York City. Pan-African Congress meets in New York City, much of its impetus spent.
1928   *Dark Princess.*
1931   Scottsboro Case begins.
1934   Breaks with NAACP, leaves editorship of *The Crisis.* Returns to Atlanta University as chairman of the Sociology Department. Mrs. Du Bois remains in Baltimore because of her hatred of the South.
1935   *Black Reconstruction in America.*
1936   Travels to Germany during the summer, sponsored by the Oberlaender Trust; returns to America January 1937.
1938   Receives honorary Ph.D. from Fisk.
1939   *Black Folk, Then and Now.*
1940   Founds and edits *Phylon. Dusk of Dawn.*
1944   Retired against his will from Atlanta. Rejoins the NAACP as director of special research.
1945   Consultant to the Founding Convention of the United Nations. Attends and is honored at Pan-African Congress in London.
1948   Fired from NAACP and given pension. Association with the Council on African Affairs begins.
1949   Makes peace pilgrimages to New York (the Cultural and Scientific Conference for World Peace, March), Paris (April), and Moscow (August).
1950   Chairman of Peace Information Center. U.S. enters Korean War. Nina Gomer Du Bois dies. Du Bois runs for U.S. Senate on American Labor Party ticket.
1951   8 February, federal grand jury indictment charges Du Bois with failure to register as an agent of a foreign principal. 14 February, marries Shirley Graham. 16 February, arraigned; 8 November, trial begins; ends five days later, case thrown out. *In Battle for Peace.*
1952   Lives at 31 Grace Court in Brooklyn, New York. 14 February, State Department refuses to issue Du Bois a passport to travel to peace conference in Rio de Janeiro.
1955   Refused passport to attend World Youth Festival in Warsaw, Poland.

Wingate College Library

1957   Bust of Du Bois unveiled in Schomburg Collection. Refused permission to attend Ghana's independence ceremonies; State Department keeps Du Bois's passport. Publishes first volume of "Black Flame" trilogy, *The Ordeal of Mansart (Mansart Builds a School,* 1959, *Worlds of Color,* 1961).

1958–
1959   Travels to USSR, China, France, England, Sweden, and East Europe. Wins Lenin Peace Prize.

1961   Travels to Ghana to work on *Encyclopedia Africana.* Joins American Communist party.

1962   *Autobiography* published in Soviet Russia.

1963   Becomes a citizen of Ghana. Dies in Accra, Ghana, 27 August. 28 August, at the March on Washington Roy Wilkins announces that Du Bois's voice was from the beginning of the century "calling you here today."

1968   *The Autogiography of W. E. B. Du Bois* published in the United States.

CHAPTER 1

The Good Years

W. E.B. DU BOIS seemed pleased to write that he was born "by a golden river and in the shadow of two great hills" in Great Barrington, Massachusetts, "in the valley of the Housatonic, flanked by" the Berkshires.[1] His birthdate, 23 February 1868, this man of history was similarly pleased to note, came five years after the Emancipation Proclamation freed his fellow black Americans in the South; the same year that Southern Negroes were granted voting rights in their native land; and one day following the annual celebration of George Washington's birthday. Thus Du Bois saw himself linked tightly to a series of events that had begun long before he was born in New England—events connected with the establishment of a democracy in the New World that would be equitable to all men and women irrespective of color.

He often described his earliest years as a happy, sometimes idyllic haven from the radical and social conflicts to which he would ultimately devote his life. Great Barrington, he claimed, was "in theory and largely in practice a democracy of the New England type" where the town attempted to solve many of its problems at town meetings that listened politely even to the village crank. Moreover, it was a town that partook of the moral zeal Du Bois considered part of the Puritan tradition, a "community which conceived itself as having helped put down a wicked rebellion for the purpose of freeing four million slaves." Though Great Barrington contained some prejudice within its nearly Edenic boundaries (as Du Bois reconstructed the town anyway) its occasional bigotry was directed more toward the new, upstart Irishmen than toward its own small, harmless, and long-standing black families. Furthermore, "the contrast between the well-to-do and the poor was not great. Living was cheap and there was little real poverty."

This land of his youth reappears throughout his numerous reminiscences as almost a mythic Happy Valley, the legendary region of plenty without pain so often sought by the American imagination. He and his mother Mary lived in a number of houses in and around town, including one owned by a black South Carolinian who wore golden earrings and fell into religious trances, and the home of his grandfather Othello Burghardt. One of his earliest memories was of the fire-tongs in Grandfather Burghardt's "sturdy, small and old fashioned" house, a memory he could refreshen when he was old since he kept the tongs with him in later years.

The great polemicist and race leader was called "Willie" as a young boy and lived seemingly, as we imagine young boys in happy valleys lived in those days we like to think were simpler than ours, but which history tells us were not—and which Du Bois makes appear simpler and certainly pleasanter than most boyhoods in the harsh century he wrote about in his histories. He tells of the time he spent racing with birds to steal local berries in the spring; he tells of just sitting on the river bank or high on the mountains overlooking the lovely valley below; but nowhere does he say that he thought cloudy, dark thoughts or brooded as he sat. Most of what scholars know of his early years emanates from evidence supplied by Du Bois himself, and after a time one wonders if his youth could have been as generally charming as he says it was—if the few upsets he remembers could have been so dangerless, for example, the time when his mother cut off his lovely curls because people from their (integrated) church were calling him a little girl.

Although blue-eyed and light in color, he was clearly recognized in town as a Negro. Always careful in his biographies to show the ways "in which Africa and Europe have been united in my family," as a young man he explained in a letter to ex-President Rutherford B. Hayes that he was "in blood, about one-half or more Negro, and the rest French and Dutch." But it was his Negro heritage that he always emphasized. In *Dusk of Dawn* he wrote that he "early began to take a direct interest in my own family as a group . . . but I did not at first think of any but my Negro ancestors." Later he gave some thought to the white strains mixed in his biracial geneology, such as his paternal great-grandfather, Dr. James Du Bois, who descended from French Huguenot farmers, and he thanked God he had no Anglo-Saxon blood. It

was, however, the black members of his family that most intrigued
him, and for a long time as a writer he would spell out the initial
"B" in his name, "since the Burghardts were black, to distinguish
his African and Afro-American derivation."[2]

Du Bois wrote often about his mother Mary, but as Julius Lester
states in *Seventh Son*, never "at length, anywhere." They were
exceptionally close, and she more than any other person was
responsible for the determined, aloof man he later became.
"Friends used to praise me," he wrote proudly in his *Autobiography*,
"for the close companionship I had with my mother." Born in
Great Barrington herself on 14 June 1831, she was lamed by a
paralytic stroke around the time Du Bois was born—or as Du Bois
explained to William T. Ingersoll, who interviewed him for
Columbia University's "Oral Memoirs" project, around the time
her husband left her. Du Bois would support her as they walked
along to amusements or on errands together, describing her as a
"dark shining bronze woman" who gave "the impression of
infinite patience" but with a "curious determination . . . concealed in her softness."

After an early romance with her cousin John that produced one
son, Idelbert, but that ended badly, she became, Du Bois said, a
"silent, repressed woman" who did housework for others before and
after she married Du Bois's father Alfred. Quiet and apparently
quietly loving and strict, she forbade her son to chew gum in the
house and placed so strong an injunction upon young Willie "never to
go into a liquor saloon or even near it" that even as an adult he felt ill
at ease while drinking in a bar. Du Bois invariably adopts a lyrical,
elegiac tone in remembering his mother that perhaps smooths over
the difficulties the two must have occasionally experienced together.
Though she seems to have been at least one source for the sexual
ignorance he discovered he possessed while at Fisk, and the emotional
inwardness he displayed much of his life, more importantly she
enabled him to grow up with a strong sense of mission and of self, to
become a tough-minded, proud black man in a world that might
have crushed him had he not been the exceptional person he became
partly through her influence upon him.

His father Alfred was another matter altogether, a shadowy,
flashy, enigmatic man in Du Bois's life whom Du Bois knew only
through his picture and through what others said about him. He
was forty-two years old when he came to the Housatonic Valley,
carefree, haughty, light of skin, and apparently shook Mary

Burghardt from the sad calm of her existence. Du Bois told several stories of his father's departure but none is very substantial. He left town probably before his son was born, though in the "Oral Memoirs" taped in 1960 Du Bois said his father left when Du Bois was a year or two old. After that, Alfred lived for a time in a town only thirty-six miles away, perhaps sent letters that possibly never arrived asking Mary to join him, or perhaps the letters did arrive and the Burghardts strongly urged Mary not to leave her home for such a skittery lightweight, and perhaps Mary gave in to her family. Whatever the reason, he left and never returned, and his son heard nothing of his life afterward and seems to have made no attempt to find out more about him. Du Bois never publicly revealed any hostility toward his father for his actions, and never recorded any feelings of rejection. The gap left by his lack of a father seems like the space that an unneeded and removed organ might leave, an organ gone before its possessor was aware of its presence. Of course, there were other male Burghardts around sometimes, or memories of them, and one of Du Bois's earliest letters contains tales of a trip he made to New Bedford, Massachusetts, in 1883, to the home of Alexander Du Bois, his grandfather. Du Bois never permitted his father's departure to shake the recollected placidity of his early years.

In Great Barrington he attended a mixed Sunday school, played marbles, "ducks on a rock," had as his first job the task of filling a few store stoves with coal, in fact, according to his second wife, Shirley Graham, "had an unusually happy childhood . . . for a black child born in the United States." He considered himself "fortunate" to have been "born in that particular place." Awareness of racial distinctions, he said, "gradually crept into my life," but he claims the distinctions made him feel only "exhaltation and high disdain," and that "not until high school was I made dimly aware that my color made any difference."[3] In retrospect he perceived himself during these years as a young New England boy growing up, aware of his African heritage but strongly molded too as his mother before him had been by the Puritan emphasis upon emotional restraint, disciplined behavior, dedication to high ideals and to one's chosen calling.

Since Great Barrington had at most half a hundred black citizens, Du Bois was one of the few black students in the school system (which had one black teacher) and experienced few instances of racial bigotry which caused him embarrassment.

Once a white girl new to town refused to exchange calling cards with him and her refusal was racially motivated. Another time he fought a white boy who had been bullying him; however, he was careful to state that the fight had no racial basis. He was early identified as an exceptionally bright student, and was encouraged by the principal, Frank Hosmer, to take courses preparing him for college—advice given few Great Barrington students, white or black. The mother of one chum bought his Greek books for him, and others in the town aided in what seems to have been a community project to permit the boy to obtain the best education the system could offer.

He appears to have glided easily between the white world and the black in these years. Nearly all his school friends were white, but he also sold and wrote for the *New York Globe*, a black newspaper. Du Bois's first published journalism reveals a competent if somewhat precociously hortatory style for a fifteen-year-old boy. In one column he urged colored men to join the local temperance society, in another he berated them for not using their vote wisely to advance other colored men in public office. Elsewhere he lamented the lack of local black businessmen. He also wrote of candy pulls and sleigh rides, and informed his readers that "those intending to replenish their libraries are advised to consult the *Globe* correspondent before so doing."

He was displaying as he grew up what he later termed his best virtue (grit) and his worst fault (sensitiveness) as a poor boy climbing what he had been trained to think of as the ladder of success, and nothing shook him from his puritanic faith in the efficacy of combining "ability and hard work" to reach the top.[4] His graduation oration was on Wendell Phillips, the New England abolitionist and later, socialist. He was entering, he thought, a world of Progress spelled with a capital P and felt that nothing could stop him from conquering that world.

Local churches and townspeople contributed money to send him not to Harvard as he wished, but to Fisk, the black school in Tennessee. They have been criticized for this decision but it seems not to have been inspired by racism. The local high school was feared not really adequate to prepare students for Harvard and had sent few graduates to any university. The town felt that whatever his mission might be, young Willie Du Bois could better serve his own and his race's interests where his race seemed to need the most help, in the South.

His mother died before he left for Fisk. Du Bois said that he felt "gladness to see her at peace at last" and "half-guilt" realizing that now he could "begin life without forsaking mother." She and Great Barrington had prepared him as well as they could. Now, he felt, the direction his life would take was up to him.

I   A Negro, a Student

Fisk introduced him to a totally new world, or rather to two worlds, one Southern and white, the other black. The first shocked and appalled him, the other shocked him also, but gave him many compensatory pleasures and satisfactions. Nashville, Tennessee, where Fisk is located, brought Du Bois into close and dangerous contact with a violently racist society for the first time. Shortly after his arrival, while he was walking along the street, he brushed against a white woman. He begged her pardon and she spat out at him, "how dare you speak to me, you impudent nigger!"[5] He experienced also directly the systematic segregation the South was becoming more and more locked into, which would grow worse and which life in Great Barrington had not prepared him for at all.

But he felt rewarded by the rich world of blackness he plunged into. His immediate family had been black, and he had occasionally seen and been thrilled by large crowds of Negroes enjoying each other's company; once, for example, he had come upon a massive picnic for black people in New Bedford, Massachusetts. But now, at Fisk, he was living daily with young black men and women, exchanging ideas with them, sharing their problems and sometimes their pleasures. At Fisk he says he was "thrilled to be for the first time among so many people of my own color or rather of such various and extraordinary colors," people bound to him "by new and exciting external ties." There was also a less enjoyable side to his contact with these vital black young men and women that Du Bois did not write very much about until he was an old man. While intellectually he was equal if not superior to any of them, physically the New England way of life his mother and town imposed upon him had left him inexperienced. The students were much more sexually advanced than Du Bois, who felt "precipitated into a region, with loose morals among black and white, while I actually did not know the physical difference between men and women." He was jeered at for his ignorance at first, then pitied. His first sexual experience he describes as a "rape" with him as the victim.

If Fisk was an emotional shock to the young Du Bois, intellectually it seems to have been exactly what he needed. Its curriculum was relatively liberal especially for a Negro school, for as Julius Lester points out, "it was not training laborers and workers for the white South, it was training leaders of the race." Du Bois describes his white teachers (the faculty was not integrated) as excellent and sometimes inspiring, and he left the school with a good knowledge of Greek, of classic works of art such as Sophocles's *Antigone* (which emphasizes the moral imperative of the individual to stand against a spiritually corrupt state), and an adequate knowledge of math and some sciences. And at Fisk Du Bois first realized what it meant to be a Negro in a white dominated land.

While an undergraduate Du Bois sent letters to Harvard stating his desire to enter that university and explaining that he was black and poor and would need financial aid. Hosmer, his old principal from Great Barrington, together with President Cravath at Fisk and several other Fisk professors, sent supporting letters. Du Bois was awarded a Price Greenleaf grant and entered Harvard in the fall of 1888. Harvard deepened him intellectually and intensified his awareness of his own blackness. Whereas in Great Barrington he was outgoing and enjoyed playing boys' games with his pals, at Harvard he consciously avoided contact, intimate or otherwise, with whites. He was becoming careful and aloof: "I did not seek white acquaintances, I let them make the advances, and they therefore thought me arrogant." His self-isolation resulted partly from his own desires, and partly from Harvard's racism. He was especially disappointed that he was excluded from the Glee Club because he was black. He always respected Harvard for nourishing his ravenous intellect, but even as an old man accustomed to (though never accepting) racial insults he was rankled that in later years the school never invited him to deliver a lecture there nor honored him as had so many other universities outside America.[6]

If institutional Harvard did not recognize Du Bois's sensitive spirit as it would have were he white, the faculty, by his account, provided him with an excellent education. He took his B.A. there in 1890, his M.A. in 1891, and his Ph.D. in 1895. Professors Albert Bushnell Hart in history and William James in philosophy were among the teachers who recognized his potential and also provided him with some personal guidance and support. "James with

his pragmatism and . . . Hart with his research method" turned
Du Bois from "philosophic speculation, to the social sciences" as
the proper field in which to develop his evolving plans for the
Negro. Though at Harvard "Karl Marx was mentioned, only to
point how thoroughly his theses had been disproven," professors
such as Hart and James and George Santayana and Josiah Royce
provided Du Bois, with their emphasis upon rigorous testing of
ideas and equally careful articulation of one's theories based upon
close observation of data, with a technique that would enable him
to establish his own radical critique of white society.

Du Bois's social life during his Harvard years was spent in the
black community, where he acted as gregariously as he was
withdrawn in the white. He was once engaged, and found time to
act in amateur theatricals such as a production titled "Sampson
and Delilah, or the Duke, the Duck and the Devil." Life was not
all academic grind, and though Harvard was not the succession of
triumphs he liked later to imagine it as having been,[7] he emerged
from the experience tougher and smarter and perhaps even more
sensitive to bigotry than when he entered. His goal in life was still
to lead his people forward, but how best to hit his target he was
still working out. He did not doubt that "what the white world
was doing, its goals and ideals . . . were quite right. What was
wrong was that I and people like me and thousands of others who
might have my ability and aspiration, were refused permission to
be a part of this world."

II *The Wanderer*

The next step he took intellectually would show the white world
how wrong they were in denying blacks a place in their world. He
would clearly demonstrate to the whites how their racist policies
were not only immoral but politically impractical. To prepare
himself to produce proof of how failure to halt the slave trade and
slavery operated fiercely against the commonweal, he felt he
needed further study and travel in Europe. His two-year stay
there, starting in the summer of 1892, "modified profoundly my
outlook on life and my thought and feeling toward it." He traveled
widely, had a romance with a German woman he calls "Dora,"
experienced the joy in France of feeling less color prejudice than
"anywhere else in the world," learned too to carry a cane at
Friederich Wilhelm University in Berlin. More significantly, he

took courses there under Gustave Schmoller and Adolph Wagner and others which revealed to him with greater clarity than ever before the connections between economics, history, and sociology, and enabled him to "see the race problem in America, the problem of the peoples of Africa and Asia, and the political development of Europe as one." He delighted in the Europe years as he did not delight in the time spent at Harvard. He drank beer and listened to *Tannhäuser* and to discussions of Karl Marx and reveled in the deepness of European culture. But he knew he could not stay there and wallow in it. A year before he left for home he wrote to the scholarship fund that was supporting him that his plan was to return to America and teach in a Negro university, to build up a department of history and social science, to "collect capable young Negro students" and "to study scientifically the Negro question past and present with a view to its best solution."[8] On his twenty-fifth birthday, feeling lonely and perhaps prophetic, he confided to himself no less grandiose but more romantic plans: "to make a name in science, to make a name in literature and thus raise my race . . . . I wonder what will be the outcome? Who knows?"

Du Bois's return to "nigger-hating" America disillusioned him but did not plunge him into the despair it might have had he been less emotionally disciplined and intellectually resourceful. He secured a job at Wilberforce University in Ohio for the fall of 1894 (turning down Booker T. Washington at Tuskeegee) and stayed there two not totally satisfactory years. He taught classical languages mainly, not the best use of his talents. He clashed often with the school's conservative black administration. Though he felt had he remained he could have helped build the college into something better, he wanted to work more actively at his dream. Knowing he was "cocky and self-satisfied," he knew too he was a hard worker and brutally frank. He felt he was pounding at a stone wall and did not want to compromise his ideals by staying at Wilberforce. He did not want to engage in futile battles and die spiritually, so he knew he could not stay.

Before he left in 1896 he met and married Nina Gomer, who would be his wife for fifty-three years. Their marriage he always described as a good one even though he "was literally frightened into" it, apparently because he felt intimidated by the sexual advances he received at the school. He would later write little about his wife although he was quite devoted to her. But beneath the surface of their genteel relationship were empty or dark recesses he never really investigated when he wrote about himself, probably because of his reticence and because he revered his wife's memory and did not want to open to the world his private heart. Nonetheless, it is apparent that their relationship was lacking at certain points important to Du Bois. She seems not to have shared in his work through her own lack of desire and perhaps through his own abrasive and intense self-involvement. And he admitted that her "life-long training as a virgin, made it almost impossible for her ever to regard sexual intercourse as not fundamentally indecent." Du Bois was a passionate man, cool as he may have appeared on the surface, and Nina's lack of warmth must have hurt him, though it made him no less committed to the success of their marriage.

Passion and commitment also distinguished Du Bois's first two major publications, each restrained by the academic discipline needed to produce sound and meaningful scholarship. Both books aimed at his early ideal of proving to the white world that its treatment of Negroes was vicious and socially inexpedient.

CHAPTER 2

"To Make a Name in Science"

I   *The Moral Historian*

DU BOIS'S first book, *The Suppression of the African Slave-Trade to the United States of America, 1638–1870*, was published in 1896 and is still used as a basic treatment of its subject. It was for its time a thoroughly if not exhaustively researched formal historical study remarkable for the sureness of its author's style and for the clarity of its fresh insights. It was also the first large chunk of what would become Du Bois's lifetime literary and personal task of rehabilitating the history of black people in Africa and America, of establishing a usable past for them in their constant, daily struggle to achieve a decent future.

Suppression appeared two years after Congress repealed the Civil Rights Act of 1866, just one year after Booker T. Washington's Atlanta Exposition address, and the same year as the Supreme Court's now notorious *Plessy* v. *Ferguson* decision which in effect denied that Jim Crow segregation in the South was illegal and which accepted the "separate but equal" concept that would be used to further subjugate Negroes North and South for over half a century. The cool, already magisterial tone that young Du Bois employed throughout most of what had been his Harvard Ph.D. dissertation could not have been easy for him to attain. Its use was devastatingly effective in treating an issue so hot to him and so dead to many Americans whose knowledge of slavery was conditioned not so much by the nightmares of *Uncle Tom's Cabin* that their parents had brooded over, as by the pastoral fantasies of dreamy historians such as Thomas Nelson Page who, in *The Old South* (1892), wrote that though "slavery in any form shocks the sensibilities of this age . . . surely this banjo-playing life was not so dreadful a lot for those just rescued from the cannibalism of the Congo."

Du Bois's subject was what Page termed the "rescue" of Africans. In his preface to the first edition he said "this monograph proposes to set forth the efforts made in the United States of America, from early Colonial times until the present, to limit and suppress the trade in slaves between Africa and these shores." His study assumed that any practice connected to the institution of slavery was morally indefensible. The spine of his book's argument is that some Americans recognized early both the practical dangers and ethical unacceptability of slavery, but that at no time prior to the Civil War was sufficient political power exerted to eliminate the slave trade. Around the time of the Revolutionary War and our nation's founding, a prime opportunity existed to outlaw the trade, but partly through moral inertia and partly through lack of political foresight, this opportunity was not grasped. Thereafter as the Cotton Kingdom grew it literally devoured slaves and increased the need for fresh imports. Proslavery defenders whose voices seemed quieter during the 1770s when slavery looked less financially attractive, became increasingly loud and strident as cotton markets and cotton technology bloomed in the late 1780s. The chance to stop slavery through political debate passed, and, according to Du Bois, as long as slavery existed so too would a significant slave trade to America.

Though eventually legal measures were instituted which, with great difficulty, limited and, in 1807, even prohibited the importation of live human flesh from foreign ports, Du Bois contended that the slave trade never stopped until slavery stopped—and not even then, completely. Prior to Lincoln's first term, no American government attempted adequately to implement antislave trade laws. The money, court trials, blockade ships, the administrative directives necessary to stop this very profitable traffic never came close to halting the crime which Americans, through individual greed and collective governmental lassitude and connivance, were incessantly committing.

Du Bois's strategy in the book was in part forced upon him by the nature of his task which was, originally, to compose a doctoral dissertation which he then revised into a book. His tone is ever calm and reasonable, his stance seemingly that of the detached historian whose job is to martial facts and let them parade by the reader in orderly review, their direction controlled by the force of historic inevitability. His language is calm and undecorated, his prose compared to many of his later works, simple and unpassionate. But he was a historian with an underlying moral purpose: to prove to Americans how unnecessary the slave trade was. Later in his career he would attack other phases of the black experience and depict them in all their cruelty and violence. In *Suppression* he rigorously avoided portraying the bloody excesses of the beastly commerce and instead, on the surface of his text anyway, manifests a cool and comparatively unemotional intellectual manner, like that of an eighteenth-century wit. Throughout Du Bois's lifetime as a writer and scholar and a director of the NAACP's actions there often warred within him or sometimes worked hand-in-hand the passionate romantic and the glacial classicist. In his best works neither totally dominated: in *Suppression* the urgings of the romantic moralist are carried out carefully by the classical historian.

This historian believed that reasonable Americans would respond to reasonable appeals. If America could only see its follies it might not perpetuate them. This historian showed past folly so that the future would be free from racist stupidity, demonstrated the moral unreasonableness of the slave trade so that Americans would not again avoid their moral obligation to treat Negroes with total constitutional fairness. So the book is both pragmatic and idealistic. Years afterward, in responding gently to a bitter letter from the black teacher and writer Horace R. Cayton that charged him with confusing black youth with false hopes of racial harmony achieved through reasonable persuasion, Du Bois wrote, "I think you make the usual mistake of many people in minimizing the importance of careful knowledge and study of the past . . . out of the past is spawned the present and only by a study of the past can we be wise for the future." *Suppression* then is a moral history, written by Du Bois under the assumption that motivated so much of his professional life as a scholar, that (in Francis Broderick's words) "the path to reform lay in the empirical knowledge which, dispelling ignorance and misapprehension, would guide intelligent social policy. As [Du Bois] said succinctly in his diary, 'The Universe is Truth. The Best ought to be. On these postulates hang all the law and the prophets.'"[1]

As had Puritan historians such as William Bradford and Edward Johnson, he demonstrated the crimes of the wicked through chronicling their sins. God, however, was not part of the scheme he described, nor was the devil. Instead, men moved by human greed, or, unmoved through moral torpor, made speeches, passed or did not pass laws, and in each activity they performed

were measured against the ethical idealism Du Bois clearly
thought men could possess. He was, as he stated in an "Apologia"
he added to the book in 1954, "trained in the New England ethic
of life as a series of conscious moral judgments" and therefore
"continually thrown back on what men 'ought' to have done to
avoid evil consequence." As a professional historian he provided
names and dates, speeches and legal measures passed or defeated,
a rich lode of information substantiating his moral judgment,
much as the Puritan historians provided biblical texts in addition
to discussions of historical events to buttress their arguments. But
always he directed himself toward moral evaluation.

Thus he concludes in one of his final paragraphs after several
hundred pages documenting the feeble attempts to suppress the
slave trade in America, "we must face the fact that this problem
arose principally from the cupidity and carelessness of our ancestors. It was the plain duty of the colonies to crush the trade and
the system in its infancy: they preferred to enrich themselves on its
profits. It was the plain duty of a Revolution based upon 'liberty'
to take steps toward the abolition of slavery: it preferred promises
to straightforward action . . . with this real, existent, growing evil
before their eyes, a bargain of dollars and cents was allowed to
open the highway that led to the Civil War." He was a historian,
but one who assigned blame where his scholarship and moral code
taught him it lay.

He did not however in this first book write from outside the
dominant culture that he attacked. In *Suppression* Du Bois still
struck out against folly from inside the beast that committed it.
Later he would write more clearly from the perspective of the
minority oppressed. Here he identifies with the majority: for
example, he refers to "the cupidity and carelessness of *our*
ancestors." Throughout *Suppression* he quite consciously writes
not only as an American but as a representative American
connected to the power structure. In the very next paragraph to
the one just cited he says "in some respects we as a nation seem to
lack" a kind of "hard common-sense in facing the complicated
phenomena of political life . . . we have the somewhat inchoate
idea that we are not destined to be harassed with great social
questions, and that even if we are, and fail to answer them, the
fault is with the question and not with us." This role that he played
in the text of his monograph served to deflect the sharp thrust of
his attack upon the American dream that slavery was somehow an

accident imposed upon the South and continued despite Northern opposition to it because the South was trapped by a system it simply could not shed without destroying itself. What Du Bois demonstrated was that the slave trade (and the slavery it nourished) was an integral part of the South's economy and to an extent the North's, and that its continuance was possible only because those who profited from the practice strenuously opposed any attempts to curtail it, and because those who opposed the trade lacked the political strength or the moral conviction to stop it when it could have been stopped without ruining the country's economy. In this critique of American political morality Du Bois wrote as a fellow American, presumably equally tainted with guilt. While his stance may have made his criticism more palatable to the educated, essentially conservative academic audience he wrote for, the posture was one he would not assume again in a major work.

Nor would he again in a major work be as seemingly dispassionate toward his material as he is in *Suppression*. A doctoral dissertation is traditionally cool and reasonable and unemotional, and that partly accounts for Du Bois's relatively restrained tone throughout his book. But as the skilled poet makes the traditional form of the sonnet work for him or her, so did Du Bois fulfill the conventional academic requirements of disinterested, objective, aesthetically unspectacular writing and make these requirements an effective force for presenting his facts and opinions. For example, early in the book he offers as a good statistician might the following details: "The exact proportions of the slave-trade to America can be but approximately determined. From 1680 to 1688 the African Company sent 249 ships to Africa, shipped there 60,783 Negro slaves, and after losing 14,387 on the middle passage, delivered 46,396 in America." He does not here, nor does he elsewhere, describe the horrors of the middle passage but simply and effectively notes that 14,387 Africans were lost enroute from Africa to the New World: by his reckoning in eight years 14,487 kidnapped Africans were killed out of 60,783. The bare numbers are chilling.

Throughout the text he often employs sober academic language that contrasts dramatically with the terrifying events he is alluding to. Du Bois was still a passionate writer but here his passion derives force from its subterranean understatement. Across the grid of his tightly organized, chronologically arranged, neatly titled succession of chapters and subchapters (chapter 5, "The Period of the Revolution, 1774-1787"; chapter 6, "The Federal Convention, 1787") he nailed fact by fact the fierce evidence he accumulated. His structure was a model of academic form, but that form contained a bitter condemnation of white America. His language was often equally formal, sometimes almost elegant, as he ironically described acts of moral dereliction in measured tones. "South Carolina," he calmly states, "was the first Southern state in which the exigencies of a great staple crop rendered the rapid consumption of slaves more profitable than their proper maintenance." In other words, in South Carolina it was cheaper to work slaves to death than to maintain them. His phrasing is professional and lofty, but his harsh point is brutally clear.

Since Du Bois felt that if he could only reach American society with his clear facts and persuasive arguments he could convince it to admit the American Negro into its communities as equal citizens, he was careful to note instances of white help in the fight for civil justice. He quoted from the protest of some Friends in Germantown, Pennsylvania in 1688: "Now, tho they are black, we cannot conceive there is more liberty to have them slaves, as it is to have other white ones. There is a saying, that we shall doe to all men like as we will be done ourselves; making no difference of what generation, descent or colour they are." And he told of a sea captain arrested in Massachusetts early in the 1640s whose collection of slaves was sent back to Africa, since according to law only "lawful Captives taken in just warres, & such strangers as willingly selle themselves or are sold to us" could be brought into the colony. At the same time he was prompt to relate that "the temptation of trade slowly forced the colony from this high moral ground." And in the end he attributes the crime of slavery to white venality. "The American slave-trade finally came to be carried on principally by United States capital, in United States ships, officered by United States citizens, and under the United States flag."

He also did not fail to recognize how blacks themselves attacked the slave system when they could. Specifically, he showed that much legislation attempting to suppress the trade was a direct result of black agitation. In insisting upon the significance of black militancy he was introducing to many of his readers a new interpretation of black history. Sometimes the Negroes whose struggles he brought to light were relatively unknown and neglected figures, such as the slave Cato whose insurrection at Stono,

North Carolina, "caused such widespread alarm that a prohibitory duty of £100 was immediately laid." In the instance of Toussaint L'Ouverture and his rebellion in Haiti, Du Bois rehabilitated what he considered an ill-understood leader of his people whom Southern detractors had formerly portrayed as a bombastic and murderous fool. For Du Bois, fear of a rebellion similar to Toussaint's attack upon colonialism was one of the main reasons state and federal legislators tried to curtail the slave trade. "Spurred by the tragedy of the West Indies, the United States succeeded by state action in prohibiting the slave trade from 1789 to 1803, in furthering the cause of abolition, and in preventing the fitting out of slave-trade expeditions in United States ports." Du Bois was constantly keen to demonstrate how black Americans had played a powerful and active role in determining many aspects of American history, not the least of which was their role in stopping slavery once and for all.

Suppression told about moral defeat, however, more than it told about moral victory. Du Bois's attitude beneath the skin of his historian's neutral objectivity is exasperation, for he believed that the slave trade and with it slavery could have been abolished much earlier and without the painful bitterness and bloodshed of the Civil War. Typically, though he was writing about an area of American life filled with injustice and moral depravity, he still felt strongly that people could have behaved otherwise and better, that within the human mass resided ethical resources that could have changed the course of history. Throughout his life he never for very long seemed to lose this feeling, an amazing feature in the character of a man so often humiliated by the rabid inhumanity of racism.

According to Du Bois the slave trade was ripe for destruction, and with it slavery itself, around the time of the Federal Convention of 1787. Opposition to the trade, whether from high moral values or self interest, was strong. Slavery itself was not as profitable as it had been. But as a Connecticut delegate to the Convention said, "it was better to let the Southern States import slaves than to part with those states." Further, as Luther Martin wrote in a letter to his constituents in Maryland that Du Bois quotes, "I found the *Eastern States*, not withstanding their *aversion to slavery*, were very willing to indulge the Southern States . . . providing the Southern States would, in their turn, gratify them, by laying no restriction on navigation acts."

Although Du Bois condemns the shortsightedness of the bargain struck at the Convention by Northern and Southern commercial concerns, supposedly in the interest of national well-being, he permits his contemporary sources to underscore the terrible irony of this compact that would in time play its part in the nearly complete rupture of the very government it was meant to preserve—that at a convention supposedly distributing the newly won fruits of freedom over the land, so immoral a deal would be consummated denying freedom to black Americans. "Centinel [*sic*]," writing to his Quaker readers in Pennsylvania, commented that failure to free the Negroes was "especially scandalous and inconsistent in a people, who have asserted their own liberty by the sword, and which dangerously enfeebles the districts wherein the laborers are bondsmen."

Thereafter, support for slavery hardened in the South and with it support for the slave trade. The fact seemed to be, as Du Bois quotes Senator Early of South Carolina, that "a large majority of people in the Southern States do not consider slavery as even an evil." Manstealing was not really a serious crime, it was at most a "misdemeanor." No wonder that the punishment for being caught engaging in the traffic was usually so slight after 1807. If the punishment were made too severe, juries would not return verdicts of guilty, and informants would not bear witness. Along with Senator Stanton of Rhode Island, many legislators could not "believe that a man ought to be hung for only stealing a negro." The utterance sounds like a very bad joke with its emphasis upon "only." Du Bois did not need to underscore the remark's fatuousness, he needed simply to set it down along with the words of other federal legislators who debated exactly what penalties should be imposed for those who broke the law of 1807 prohibiting the importing of slaves from outside the country. Nor does he ever lose control of his emotions though he must have been enraged in reviewing the material he had collected. The logical, balanced structure he employs, the divided and subdivided sections ("60. Enforcement of the Act . . . . 61. Evidence of Continuance of the Trade . . . . 62. Apathy of the Federal Government") contain and direct his rage. His emotions are bound up in his facts and thrown upon the object of his attack, the moral cowardice of the American government in suppressing—or rather in not suppressing—the slave trade.

Nearly always his language is restrained and formal, though the information he expressed might contain a brutal condemnation of those who permitted the trade to continue and who profited by it. "The fitting out of slavers became a flourishing business in the United States, and centered at New York City," he writes simply, "as though the slave trade were just another industry rooting itself in American mercantile life." As his indictment calmly proceeds along lines of academic inquiry he has carefully established, the moral depravity of the system he is describing becomes increasingly apparent, creating a kind of rhetorical pressure as his calm scholar's language portrays the ever-growing entanglement of slavery and American politics. He narrates through the use of historical detail a story whose plot becomes more and more horrific while his tone of voice remains steady and unemotional. He does not become more outraged himself, but he does provide information that is more and more outrageous.

Because the slave trade was not vigorously attacked in 1783 and 1787 when the time was ripe for its destruction, it lingered and grew strong until its termination risked the destruction of the nation. The Civil War ended slavery and virtually ended the slave trade, and for Du Bois, the war was fought over the fate of black men and women, not over state's rights. As a moralist and as a historian Du Bois pointed out in his concluding chapter called "The Lesson for Americans" what his countrymen should learn from his examination of the slave trade. He was writing of a contemporary problem when he wrote of slavery, so his message was especially apposite. In his time, although slavery did not exist as a legally sanctioned system, it remained as a model of treatment for suppressed Negro Americans in the South and North.

"It behooves the United States," Du Bois begins his savagely, politely understated final paragraph, "in the interest both of scientific truth and of future social reform, carefully to study such chapters in her history as that of the suppression of the slave-trade. The most obvious question which this study suggests is: How far in a State can a recognized moral wrong safely be compromised?" Du Bois answers his question as coolly and courteously as he asked it, with but one phrase (which I italicize though he does not) to suggest the strength of the bitter accusation his measured words contain: America's lesson was not to permit "through carelessness and *moral cowardice* any social evil to grow." Then in his last two sentences he lashes out still politely but relentlessly against the spiritually corrupt, for the final time insisting upon how great social evils grow and fester at the same time through neglect founded in moral sloth. "No persons would have seen the Civil War with more surprise and horror than the Revolution of 1776; yet from the small and apparently dying institution of their day arose the walled and castled Slave-Power. From this we may conclude that it behooves," he says repeating the polite word with which he began his final statement, "it behooves nations as well as men to do things at the very moment when they ought to be done."

His last sentence is a masterpiece of simple understatement. Following as it does almost two hundred pages of closely reasoned argument and vast collections of statistics and source citations, it hits a powerful note of exhortation made even more impressive by what could be interpreted as its naiveté but which after so much proof is actually its stark pragmatism.

Suppression of the Slave-Trade was the product of a very young scholar, but clearly not apprenticeship work. Du Bois does not seem constrained by the dissertationlike format he follows, rather he uses the form to contain and focus his powers as a writer, to restrain the emotionalism that could aid or hinder him as a craftsman: like the fire it resembled in so many ways, his emotionalism was a good literary servant to Du Bois, but a poor master. In *Suppression of the Slave-Trade* he uses his emotional commitment to his subject but does not let it use him. The work is still a standard among historians of the period (as such it is referred to in Kenneth Stampp's classic 1956 study *The Peculiar Institution*). Historians vary in weighing the value of its individual components, of course, and some naturally dispute its general perspective. Professor A. Norman Klein says in his introduction to the most recent edition of the text that the "economic analysis of the slave-trade and its eventual suppression is at times naive" and that Du Bois paid too little attention to the fact that the American brand of slavery was unique in that it allowed for significant growth internal to the system through a relatively high birthrate. However, Klein concludes that Du Bois's book remains "a classic in its field, a monument both to his researches and his talent for selecting critical questions and answers."

The book was innovative in many ways, for example, in insisting upon the role Negro slave insurrections played in shaping abolitionistic attitudes. Throughout, Du Bois unsentimentally operated on the institutions of slave trading and slavery like a surgeon dissecting diseased organs, cutting away the fat of decades of romanticized historical rhetoric: "The main difference in motive," he says coldly, "between the restrictions which the planting and the farming colonies put on the African slave-trade, lay in the fact that the former limited it mainly from fear of insurrection, the latter mainly because it did not pay." Du Bois wrote in the 1954 "Apologia" to his book that he was disturbed by the "ignorance" his analysis revealed about "the word of Freud and Marx." He also feared that he "missed the strength of the economic reasons for the failure to stop the trade," but concluded that he was "proud to see that at the beginning of my career I made no more mistakes than apparently I did." His pride was justified.

II   The Philadelphia Negro *and Humane Sociology*

Infrequently read now and at the time of its publication read only by academic professionals, Du Bois's second book, *The Philadelphia Negro* (1899), is actually one of his most impressive and fascinating. Functioning in the work primarily as an urban anthropologist presenting a panorama of data as scientifically collected as the slender financial resources at his command permitted, Du Bois also managed to fuse his findings with his own personal vision and perspective. The resulting combination of objective reporting with Du Bois's passionate insight and sometimes devastating wit, was as rare when the book was first published as it is now.

The original impetus for Du Bois's study came from Susan B. Wharton, at the time a member of the Executive Committee of the Philadelphia Settlement, who in a letter to the provost of the University of Pennsylvania stated a desire to work out some "plan for the better understanding of the colored people, especially of their position in this city . . . a plan to obtain a body of reliable information as to the obstacles to be encountered by the colored people in their endeavor to be self-supporting, etc." Du Bois's interests and proven scholarship made him the logical choice for the job, and his realization that Wilberforce was a dead end for him undoubtedly whetted his desire to begin the great and burdensome task he was being asked to perform single-handedly. In August 1896, he moved into a one-room apartment in the worst section of the city with his bride of three months and lived there for a year collecting information by trekking from house to house, tenement to tenement, interviewing, he said, over 5,000 inhabitants, collating questionnaires, systematically investigating the history of black Philadelphia so that his study of present-day Negro life there would not exist in a historical vacuum.

Despite certain mean ironies connected with his academic relationship with the university, he was happy performing what he considered exciting and meaningful work. The university faculty apparently recognized his color along with his scholarship, for he had no contacts with students and very little with faculty members (even those in his own department), and his name was omitted from the college catalog. In *Darkwater* he says he was paid $600 and in his *Autobiography* $900 a year for his efforts,[2] and he was given after some discussion and debate the unusual title of "assistant instructor." But he was doing what he wanted to do. Though his salary permitted him to spend only five dollars for his wife's Christmas, plus fifteen cents for a Christmas tree, the time was a good one for them both.

His basic method of research was simple and hard. He knocked at the door of each domicile he could locate in the Seventh Ward, sat down with whomever answered his knock, and asked questions for ten minutes to an hour. His lengthy questionnaire was designed to gather precise information and to note inconsistent or misleading answers. Most of his respondents were "prompt and candid," though when he received what he considered a false response he "inserted no answer at all, or one which seemed approximately true." He would also often obtain corrective information from neighbors. His objectives were as he stated them at the outset of his book, "to ascertain something of the geographical distribution of this race, their occupations and daily life, their homes, their organizations, and above all, their relation to their million white fellow-citizens." He was at this time still determined that the "Negro problem was . . . a matter of systematic investigation and intelligent understanding. The world was thinking wrong about race, because it did not know. The ultimate evil was stupidity. The cure for it was knowledge based on scientific investigation."[3]

One of the basic assumptions of Du Bois's historical narrative restated what he had already concluded in *The Suppression of the Slave-Trade*, that proper action shortly after the Revolutionary War could have alleviated or prevented much of the racial strife that continued increasingly to plague America throughout the latter years of the nineteenth century. "Sporadic cases of talent" appeared in Philadelphia's black community, such as Richard Allen and Absalom Jones, who formed the Free African Society in 1787 when they and other black communicants were segregated from whites in St. George's Episcopal Church. Each man ultimately formed his own church, and, as Du Bois pointed out, Allen's African Methodist Episcopal Church evolved eventually into a powerful Negro institution with over 500,000 members in Du Bois's day. "The condition of the Negroes of the city in the last decades of the eighteenth and the first two decades of the nineteenth century, though without doubt bad, slowly improved." A kind of insurance society administered by and for Negroes evolved, and more and more Negro children were going to school. In general blacks seemed to have been viewed grudgingly as an integral part of the community though still inferior. In the War of 1812 black citizens proved their loyalty by raising 2,500 volunteer soldiers in response to "an alarm felt at the approach of the British." But the equal opportunity so passionately dreamed of and in some instances fought for never arrived.

Advances made by individual Negroes such as Allen and Jones or the relatively prosperous caterers Robert Bogle, Peter Augustin, and the Prossers meant little improvement for most Philadelphia blacks, who continued to be poor, badly educated, sometimes brutalized by mobs, and almost always restricted in the jobs available to them. Du Bois tells of one white riot in August 1834, apparently triggered by anti-abolitionist sentiment, during which white mobs invaded black neighborhoods, destroyed thirty-one houses and two churches, and killed Stephen James, "an honest, industrious colored man." The following year another white mob decided to punish the black community because a Cuban slave named Juan had murdered his master. The mob surrounded an armed group of Negroes who had barricaded themselves in a house until, as Du Bois calmly narrates the story, "the mayor and recorder finally arrived . . . and after severely lecturing the Negroes (!) induced them to depart."

In this early section of the book Du Bois remains calm and even in his tone, and only rarely (as when he places the exclamation point here after the word "Negroes") adds any bitter commentary of his own. The conclusion to his historical summary is understated, in keeping with the neutral and unimpassioned voice he adopted throughout most of his narrative. "It cannot be denied that the main results of the development of the Philadelphia Negro since the war have on the whole disappointed his well-wishers." His phrasing in this summation is ambiguous, since his statement can mean either that the Negro has himself developed poorly, or that the development permitted the Negro has been inadequate. This ambiguity accurately reflects a split attitude toward the predicament of the Negro that Du Bois maintains throughout most of his book, for in *The Philadelphia Negro* Du Bois seems disappointed both with elements in the Negro mass and with the white society that surrounded, indeed nearly engulfed, the black community.

The remaining bulk of the book establishes, by presenting statistics and analyses, the network of socioeconomic conditions which conspired to maintain Negro life at the very lowest level of health and opportunity in the city. Du Bois's gathering of data was exhaustive. He collected evidence on every imaginable aspect of black life from obvious areas such as wages earned to more demographically esoteric topics as the proportion of rent repaid in subrent by black individuals and families (who would, for example, rent a house from its owner and in turn rent out unused rooms to lodgers). Du Bois precisely described that web of despair so familiar to anyone who has studied black life in America, and was perhaps the first to set forth the bleak statistical configurations of black urban existence in such exact and substantial and depressing detail. His statistics made clear that Philadelphia Negroes had vastly fewer educational opportunities than their white (even immigrant) counterparts, that they had vastly fewer job opportunities at all levels of work from the most menial to the professional occupations, that they committed or were arrested for committing a disproportionate number of crimes and were sent to jail more often and stayed longer than convicted white criminals, that when they worked they were paid less, and that blacks tended to die at an earlier age than whites.

III   *Reasons for Despair*

Du Bois also demonstrates how these conditions of inequality reinforce each other to drag the Negro down, as though a heavy net whose interwoven strands support each other had been thrown over the black community. Early in the book he notes the "disproportionate number of young persons . . . women between eighteen and thirty and men between twenty and twenty-five . . . an abnormal number of young untrained persons at the most impressionable age . . . when there has not been developed fully the feeling of responsibility and personal worth." This young population was undereducated, often the product of home life fragmented by the forces pressing down upon the community, frequently jobless. Further shocked by incessant and unfair competition with waves of foreign immigrants who were sustained and aided by the white society which was in many ways hostile to their fellow black Americans, it was no wonder that young (and older) Philadelphian Negroes engaged in criminal activities. "The field for exercising their talent and ambition is, broadly speaking, confined to the dining room, kitchen, and street." The "atmosphere of rebellion and discontent" that pervaded the black sections of Philadelphia, Du Bois claimed, naturally resulted from "unrewarded merit and reasonable but unsatisfied ambition" that ensured a "social environment of excuse, listless despair, careless indulgence and lack of inspiration to work."

Du Bois's statistics in ruthless columns of unemotional numbers and carefully drawn graphs form a strongly and clearly constructed foundation upon which his authoritatively delivered conclusions stand firmly. "Of 1,000 children entering the primary grade 110 go to the grammar school, ten to the high school and one to college or to a professional school." Further, that one who goes to college may learn that "it is useless to work; it is fruitless to deserve well of men; education will gain you nothing but disappointment and humiliation."

When Du Bois lists the percentage of young black men under thirty committed to Philadelphia's Easter Penitentiary for a given time span compared to the white population of the prison (66.92%) are black) he also suggests reasons to explain this disproportion, chief among which are lack of education and vocational opportunity. But he also suggests less easily verifiable reasons. The Negro environment differs, he says, from that of any class of white Americans no matter how poor or powerless. That difference he admits he cannot offer statistics on, for it is the "widespread feeling all over the land, in Philadelphia as well as in Boston and New Orleans, that the Negro is something less than an American and ought not to be much more than what he is." This ability to generalize eloquently from the basis of his own experience, this willingness to examine as a humanist levels of human feelings and values that statistics can get at only clumsily if at all, characterizes Du Bois's rare variety of sociological investigation.

Occasionally Du Bois sounds more like a black Puritan in his exhortations than a social scientist. He calls upon Negroes, for example, to engage in "work, continuous and intensive; work, although it be menial and poorly rewarded work; work, though done in travail of soul and sweat of brow." For work is "the road to salvation." A number of times he deplores the "lax moral habits of the slave regime" still observable in the "sexual looseness [that] is today the prevailing sin of the mass of the Negro population." He asks that "the homely virtues of honesty, truth and chastity must be instilled in the cradle." This is the job of black people themselves, he says, though he is careful to note that "it is hard to teach self-respect to a people whose million fellow-citizens half-despise them." To today's readers some of Du Bois's criticisms of Negro life may seem like white paternalism: "The Negro has much to learn of the Jew and Italian, as to living within his means and saving every penny from excessive and wasteful expenditures."

Certainly some of his attitudes here stem from the New England heritage that was so strong a part of him, but he was also motivated by a need to instill black self-pride in a people whose pride was constantly under attack by social forces they could do very little about—yet he wanted black people to control their lives when they could. He wanted them to exhibit choice, and not simply submit to environmental pressures. All his life he attacked deterministic theories of social evolution such as those popularized in his own day by Herbert Spencer, who argued that those who survived and prospered were the most fit to survive, that those who fell by the way did so because social forces as relentless as forces of nature (such as natural selection) determined their destruction.

Social Darwinism was always anathema to Du Bois who saw in its theories another rationale for justifying the oppression and subjugation of black Americans and of what he termed colored races throughout the world. He bitterly opposed the kind of sociological outlook exemplified by the title of William Graham Sumner's 1894 essay "The Absurd Effort to Make the World Over." Du Bois felt that life was bad for Negroes in America because social forces controlled and directed by whites made their life bad, but he did not want to treat black people as simply passive, inert organisms totally lacking in responsibility for their situation. He always identified attempts which black Americans made to help themselves, and he pointed out where they were failing to strive for self-improvement. He would have agreed with his ex-mentor William James that "calling a thing bad means, if it means anything at all, that the thing ought not to be, that something ought to be in its stead. Determinism . . . virtually defines the universe as a place in which what ought to be is impossible."[4] So he felt that Philadelphia blacks could in some ways direct their lives, for good or bad; though he was careful to direct his harshest jeremiads toward the white society whose sins and guilt far exceeded the relatively minor failures of his fellow Negroes: "How long," he asks, "can a city teach its black children that the road to success is to have a white face? How long can a city do this and escape the inevitable penalty?"

Du Bois appeals to human reason and enlightened self-interest to solve the problems resulting from discrimination against blacks in Philadelphia. He does this even while recognizing that "one of the great postulates of the science of economics—that men will seek their economic advantage—is in this case untrue . . . if it involves association . . . with Negroes." Especially he stresses the need for more and better jobs for Negroes to solve that "question of economic survival [which] is the most pressing of all questions." Like Booker T. Washington he called for a "special effort to train Negro boys for industrial life" since "in the long run this would be best for all concerned." But unlike Washington he openly declared the need sternly to attack any "organized or covert opposition to Negro workmen."

What he describes in *The Philadelphia Negro* as the condition of black life in the city seems a closed system locking black men and women into an encompassing cycle of inferiority whose downward thrust was so strong and powered from so many sources that no mere tampering with the social machine would cause it to redirect black people as a class into the mainstream of American life where they might expect the same possibilities of social success and failure as white Americans. The probable reason why Du Bois did not strongly and consistently acknowledge the virtually inescapable downward path black life in Philadelphia seemed destined to take unless some very radical changes were effected in the political and social structure dominating America, was that he had not yet himself accepted the clear conclusion of the evidence he had collected. Trained by some of the best minds in Europe and America in the primacy of reason in analyzing society and obtaining solutions to the most complicated of problems; the recipient himself of American meliorism; an American living in a country whose obvious raw power was becoming more and more manifest as the end of one century of Western progress was preparing to lead directly into another upwardly spiraling epoch of technological accomplishment; Du Bois could not yet accept what his book throughout its discussions and graphs and tables illustrated. When he claims in his concluding chapter called "A Final Word" that "Negroes must cultivate a spirit of calm, patient persistence in their attitude," that "social reforms move slowly and yet when Right is reinforced by calm but persistent Progress we somehow all feel that in the end it must triumph," he is really ignoring the logical conclusions of his data. He is also forgetting what the history he compiled demonstrated: American society was not always reasonable, and when self-interest and prejudice clashed within white society, prejudice often triumphed.

But his book presented more than enough evidence to permit readers to construct their own conclusions about what black life in Philadelphia was like and what were the chances of change from within the system.

IV   How the Other Half Lives

Also greatly contributing to the book's value was Du Bois's ability to dramatize the vital black world from which he abstracted his graphs and tables. This talent to illuminate social theory with the bright warm light of humanity was perhaps Du Bois's special gift to academic sociology. His base of operations, the Seventh Ward, emerges from the book as real today as it must have been then, as dirty, as teeming with life, with people who either as derelicts or social strivers become not just points on a demographer's chart but real and very human creations.

The ward was perhaps the city's worst, with a number of streets described by Du Bois as "haunts of noted criminals . . . gamblers and prostitutes, and at the same time of many poverty-stricken people, decent but not energetic. . . . The corners, night and day, are filled with Negro loafers—able-bodied young men and women, all cheerful, some with good natures, open faces, some with traces of crime and excess, a few pinched with poverty." Just a few blocks away "the atmosphere suddenly changes." Here the streets have few alleys and the residences are good-sized and pleasant, and here some of the better-off Negro families live. A few are wealthy in a small way, nearly all are Philadelphia born, representing an earlier wave of emigration from the old slum section and proving that some of the black poor had improved their position in the city. Nearby is "a curious mingling of respectable working people and some of a better class with recent immigrations of the semi-criminal class from the slums," a volatile mix.

"Respectable" Negroes predominate in this neighborhood, but like Dickens's London the area is also filled with "a dangerous criminal class. They are not the low, open idlers of Seventh and Lombard, but rather the graduates of that school: shrewd and sleek politicians, gamblers and confidence men, with a class of well-dressed and partially undetected prostitutes." Du Bois generally shows how the "criminal classes" and "prostitutes" are the victims of social forces they cannot control. They serve him also as symbols of wasted Negro life, destroyed by the great white city that like some societal engine sucks its fuel from the farms and villages only to burn it up and spew it forth into the black wards.

Many of the descriptions read like vignettes from a naturalistic novel or from the muckracking journalistic literature of the day such as Jacob Riis's *How the Other Half Lives* (1890). Du Bois portrays a "ward of lodgers and casual sojourners; newly married couples" starting out who "settle down here until they are compelled by the appearance of children to move into homes of their own" if they are lucky. Sometimes we see these people in brief, bright flashes: "two little colored girls walking along South Street stopped before a gaudy pair of men's shoes displayed in a shop window." One says, "that's the kind of shoes I'd like to buy my fellow!" And that is all we learn of them, and in some ways all we need to know, for as Du Bois states, "the remark fixed their life history." Sometimes brief case histories are related sparely and soberly, without comment: "three persons in the family: a woman of thirty-four, with a son of sixteen and a second husband of twenty-six. Both the husband and son are out of work." The man is a waiter, the boy a bootblack. "They live in one filthy room, twelve feet by fourteen, scantily furnished and poorly ventilated." The woman cleans house when she can, makes "about three dollars a week. They pay twelve dollars a month for three rooms, and sub-rent two of them to other families." Food costs them about a dollar a week plus "something" for beer.

Sometimes people appear only in lists: number 18, Naudain Street: "Family of three; the man, who is decent, has broken his

leg; the wife plays policy." Du Bois's sharp eyes seem to have seen
everything precisely and sympathetically and sometimes even
comically: "an attempt was made in 1897 to count the frequenters
of certain saloons in the Seventh Ward between the hours of 8–10
on a Saturday night" by students of the Wharton School under the
direction of Dr. S. M. Lindsay. Du Bois in a straight faced manner
informs us that one saloon, watched by the intrepid scholars, was
entered by 24 white men and 102 colored men (plus two white and
three colored women). Twelve men carried liquor away, and there
were eight "drunken persons seen." At another bar "two Negro
women carried beer away in kettles; one white woman (Irish)
made two trips."

As a part of his vivid panorama of black life Du Bois also
discusses and describes black middle-class life in the Seventh Ward
and in Philadelphia. He states that the class is "curiously ham-
pered by the fact that" though they are the "aristocracy of their
own people," they "are not prepared for this role, and their own
masses are not used to looking to them for leadership." In language
we might today object to because of its paternalism, though it was
simply a part of the standard terminology of Du Bois's time, he
points out the anomalous situation of this small (8.2 percent)
group of people with their fragile grasp upon material adequacy:
"the first impulse of the best, the wisest and richest is to segregate
themselves from the mass." This seems natural to Du Bois but also
totally unacceptable to any hope of black progress, for "however
laudable an ambition to rise may be, the first duty of an upper
class is to serve the lowest classes." This idea, more baldly clothed
in bourgeois language than will later be ordinary with Du Bois,
states his concept of the "Talented Tenth," the successful Negroes
whose duty he felt was to employ their position and resources to
help raise the masses left behind them at the bottom of the
American ladder of prosperity.

Poor as he was by white standards for a professional with his
doctorate, Du Bois was solidly a member of the black bourgeoise
at the time he wrote *The Philadelphia Negro*. He maintained a
definite attitude of *noblesse oblige* toward the poverty riddled
urban blacks. He sympathized with their plight and he commented strongly upon every injustice that he saw they were
subject to, but he was still a firm enough believer in the idea of
individual responsibility to criticize those Negroes who in his eyes
submitted to their harsh destiny through unnecessary ignorance or

laziness. His attitude to these failures was complex because at the same time that he blamed them for their waywardness he carefully documented how virtually impossible it was for Negroes to succeed on equal terms with whites in America. It is as though in his theorizing he was a liberal who felt that adjustments in the system and in Negroes' greater use of the system and of their own abilities would naturally lead to the social gains blacks needed to ensure equal access to the American Dream, but in his vision he was a radical, for what he saw was that the system simply was not working for Negroes and would not no matter how hard they tried. The system had to be changed.

Thus, for example, while he claims that in general it is not true that "foreigners and trades unions have crowded Negroes out on account of race prejudices and left employers and philanthropists helpless in the matter," he demonstrates the opposite. While he states that "undoubtedly much blame can rightly be laid at the door of Negroes for submitting rather tamely to this organized opposition" to their employment by the unions and management, he proves in his case studies and in his history of the region that opposition did occur and was invariably dealt with ruthlessly. And while he submits that the reason Philadelphia Negroes were sick so much and threw "on the community a larger number of helpless widows and orphans than either they or the city can afford" is "primarily . . . because the Negroes are as a mass ignorant of the laws of health" and because "in habits of personal cleanliness and taking proper food and exercise, the colored people are woefully deficient," nearly every section of his book proves that the Philadelphia Negroes were never given the educational or employment opportunities to enable them to become expert in personal hygiene, or if they were expert to live in an area where its practice would be meaningful and not gratuitous—as in the rat infested slums.

But it is only occasionally that Du Bois fails to show clearly the nature of the trap black Philadelphians were in and how slender were their own resources for escape. He consistently calls for black responsibility and black self-help, but increasingly as he presents his statistics his commentary becomes more pointed and urgent, calling upon the city to recognize its responsibilities. The latter sections of the book contain fewer tables and graphs and more devices for emphasizing the terrible predicament of the Philadelphia Negro, as Du Bois writes somewhat less of specific, ab-

stracted economic conditions and more about what prejudice—
hard to quantify but easy to observe—means to the human beings
who experience it, "that widespread feeling of dislike for his
blood, which keeps him and his children out of decent employment, from certain public conveniences and amusements, from
hiring houses in many sections, and in general, from being
recognized as a man."

More and more of the last quarter of the book is devoted to
catalogs that show how overwhelmed the Philadelphia Negroes
were who tried to lead a life of simple opportunity: lists telling of
jobs that could not be held by blacks, training that could not be
received, unions that could not be joined, equal wages that would
not be paid, numbers of children who could not be helped into
positions of equal footing with their white counterparts. The double
binds of being black are described. When public invitations were
issued to certain events, Negroes who went were apt to be insulted
or attacked, while Negroes who stayed home were "blamed for
indifference." Blacks who did not greet white friends on the street
were boorish, those who said hello were probably snubbed.

Rarely does the powerful and passionate voice of Du Bois break
through the statistics he collected or the lists he cunningly devised
or the melioristic rhetoric he effectively employed to suggest that
the situations he was describing could be improved. One significant occasion upon which he allows the relatively dispassionate
surface of his text to be disturbed occurs nearly at its conclusion, in
a subsection titled with deceptive simplicity "The Meaning of All
This." Here, Du Bois not dispiritedly but angrily charges that he
must judge from the pleased responses he observed to the most
recent census figures showing the decrease of black population in
Philadelphia that Negroes are the only people whose "utter
disappearance . . . from the earth [would be] greeted with ill-
concealed delight."

Following this shocking accusation, Du Bois, for perhaps the
only time in his treatise, permitted the agony of his knowledge to
overcome his strong posture of a calm, reasoning sociohistorian.
Even so, his language is still formal and the structure of his
rhetoric firmly patterned into parallel syntactic and rhythmic
units. The power his prose contains here derives not simply from
linguistic devices but from the passion he contained in the earlier
passages of his book, which now bursts forth in dynamic measures. "Other centuries looking back upon the culture of the

nineteenth would have a right to suppose that if, in a land of freemen, eight millions of human beings were found to be dying of disease, the nation would cry with one voice, 'Heal them!' If they were staggering on in ignorance, it would cry 'Train them!' If they were harming themselves and others by crime, it would cry 'Guide them!' And such cries are heard and have been heard in the land; but it was not one voice and its volume has been ever broken by counter cries and echoes. 'Let them!' 'Train them like slaves!' 'Let them stagger downward!'"

This bold outburst suddenly illuminates the jagged landscape of his statistics with the sharp flare of light flowing from the future, contrasting the terrifying difference between what the present should be like, and what it is. Shortly after this imprecation Du Bois concludes his analysis of conditions among black Philadelphians with the understated call to whites for a "polite and sympathetic attitude toward these striving thousands; a delicate avoidance of that which wounds and embitters them; a generous granting of opportunity to them." Together with black efforts at self-help, he says, this response will go far to make blacks and whites understand what is implied by the other name for Philadelphia, the City of Brotherly Love. Taking into consideration all the statistics (which show such a grotesque disparity between white life and black that they seem more like expressionistic symbols of radical inequality) and commentary Du Bois has offered in his preceding pages demonstrating how shabbily Philadelphia Negroes have been treated, it is impossible not to read his concluding injunction as bitter irony.

V A Model Study

The limitations of *The Philadelphia Negro* as a sociological study and as a polemic for Negro rights are obvious and understandable in light of the slender resources Du Bois had at his command and the stage he had progressed to in his thinking: it is the work of a relatively young scholar in an academic discipline as yet unfixed in its aims and methods, the work of a perceptive observer still operating from many of the faulty basic assumptions his culture had provided him with. He admits that his questionnaire-interview method of gaining data depends in part upon the validity of what his respondents tell him about their own lives. He built into his method devices that would pick up many inaccuracies and inconsistencies, but still he realized he could not achieve information that was totally reliable. More perplexing is the conservatism of some of his elitist attitudes. "Stealing and fighting are ever the besetting sins of half-developed races," he states at one point. "There can be no doubt but that the wisest provision [for black enfranchisement after the Civil War] would have been an educational and property qualification impartially enforced against ex-slaves and immigrants" he states another time, both unwisely and undemocratically. Further, the book is filled with smug designations such as "vicious and criminal classes," "the best class of Philadelphia Negroes," and "the better class of Negroes." Even more objectionable are comments such as that referring to the influx of recently freed slaves as a "migration of barbarians," or his remark on the need to plan where to locate poor Negroes where they will not taint the well-to-do blacks: "it is not well to clean a cess-pool until one knows where the refuse can be disposed of without general harm."

Such comments are incriminating only if we forget that Du Bois was like most fellow humans a product of his environment, influenced by what he had been taught at school and in his home and what he read in books. He was not born a radical though he was born black. He grew in his thought, he evolved. He became a radical because of his black experience and because he studied poverty over and over again, and because he saw the life around him shifting into different patterns as his vision and growing imagination suggested to him what that life might be like and how it might be achieved. His vision of black life in Philadelphia is nearly always accurate even if his theorizing about that life was sometimes culture bound. In time, his theory would grow closer to his vision. That was how his mind developed. Probably the least read of Du Bois's chief works because of its bulk and its heavy statistical nature, *The Philadelphia Negro* is one of Du Bois's most important. The book demonstrates as did *The Suppression of the Slave-Trade* how well he could master a complicated academic form while bending the constraints of that form to suit his needs and talents. While presenting and interpreting great masses of sociological data with clarity, he still managed to write a compellingly interesting book pervaded though not overwhelmed by his own critical and personal insights.

Perhaps Gunnar Myrdal's opinion of the book in his study of race, *An American Dilemma* (1944), offers the most authoritative critique of Du Bois's turn-of-the-century investigation: it is, Myrdal wrote, a model study best meeting the requirements "of what a study of a Negro community should be." As an analysis of urban poverty the work was one of the earliest in America to investigate city conditions using the only recently developed techniques and perspectives of formal sociology. Appearing midway through the publication in England of Charles Booth's monumental *Life and Labour of the People in London* (seventeen volumes, 1891–1903), it became part of a tradition of important American studies such as Robert Hunter's *Poverty* (1904) and the 1910–1912 Pittsburgh Survey. Black sociology in America stems from it, as E. Franklin Frazier, St. Clair Drake, and Horace Cayton have attested to. Termed by Cayton and Drake in their *Black Metropolis* "the first important sociological study of a Negro community in the United States," the book was to be Du Bois's last major academic work for almost four decades.[5]

CHAPTER 3

"To Make a Name in Literature"

SINCE neither the University of Pennsylvania nor any other white university seemed to want the brilliant but black scholar on their regular faculty, and since Du Bois continued firm in his desire to study the "Negro problem" in America scientifically, he was pleased with the offer in 1897 of a fellow New Englander, President Horace Bumstead, to teach at Atlanta University, establish a sociology department, and oversee and shape the Atlanta University studies program. Du Bois wrote in his *Autobiography* that his "real life work was begun" at Atlanta. "Here I found myself. I lost most of my mannerisms. I grew more broadly human."

Beyond teaching—where he insisted upon the most rigorous standards of performance from himself and his students—Du Bois considered his chief professional work at Atlanta to be the series of Atlanta conferences which he grafted upon the original university studies program. The stated aim of the conferences and the annual publications they produced (which Du Bois edited) was to collect a "basic body of fact concerning the social condition of Negroes." Though not aimed toward immediate social improvement, the conferences spurred and facilitated some specific programs, such as the kindergarten system for whites and blacks (segregated) in Atlanta and the Negro Business League. The conferences were typical products of Du Bois's imagination. Highly idealistic and even grandiose in their ultimate concept (planned to stretch out well beyond Du Bois's lifetime), they were pragmatically successful in operation. Focusing on such topics as "The Social and Physical Condition of Negroes in Cities" (1897), "The Negro in Business" (1899), and "The Negro Church"(1903), they were richly informative and highly stimulating to future research, although highly uneven in the validity of their research techniques.

Du Bois's prominence as a scholar-writer increased during his tenure at Atlanta. Producing *The Souls of Black Folk* (1903), *John Brown* (1909), and *The Quest of the Silver Fleece* (published after his departure, in 1911) as his chief books, almost numberless magazine and newspaper articles, and a clutch of poems including "A Litany At Atlanta" and "The Burden of Black Women," he also found time to edit two short-lived but interesting periodicals, *The Moon* (1906) and *Horizon* (1907–1910). As he would continue to do all his life, he spoke outside the college to whomever would listen about the condition of the Negro in contemporary society, and became increasingly well known as an incisive and controversial spokesman for many American Negroes. His growing national and international reputation also stemmed from three activities he engaged in beyond those directly connected to his professional position: his work for Pan-Africanism, his conflict with Booker T. Washington, and his civil rights advocacy.

Du Bois attended his first Pan-African conference in 1900, in England, where he first heard the term "Pan-African" used by a West Indian lawyer named H. Sylvester Willams. According to Harold Isaacs, Du Bois said he "did not . . . begin actively to study Africa until 1908 or 1910 . . . and I began to get into it only after 1915."[1] But as his reminiscences in *Souls of Black Folk* prove, a memory of Africa transmitted through an African song long retained in his family had intrigued him since early childhood. After the first conference Du Bois directed or participated in five more Pan-African congresses, most of which were organized only with difficulty because of inadequate funds and political pressures exerted by western powers. The congresses called for increased independence for African nations, nearly all of which were still colonies as late as the 1945 congress in Manchester, England; stressed the need for greater unity among African states; and sought greater awareness of the common interests of black people in America, the West Indies, and Africa.

I *Africa, My Africa*

It will benefit the student of Du Bois's life to see spread out at once the extent and results of Du Bois's participation in Pan-Africanism, although this overview will necessarily involve a chronological leap through and beyond Du Bois's Atlanta years.

Most historians of the Pan-African movement—really move-ments, since it always contained factions who in significant ways disagreed with each other on aims and strategies—would proba-bly agree with Colin Legum's assessment that Du Bois was "by no means the first but perhaps the most important link between the literary and political streams of Pan-Africanism" which "for almost half a century he dominated."[2] While he was not as crucial to the movement as his accounts of its history suggest, he was surely over the years the most prominent American Negro to advance its cause and give it intellectual and political legitimacy. Certainly his speech at the 1900 London conference with its memorable phrase "the problem of the twentieth century is the problem of the color line" provided Pan-Africanism with a rhetorical visability it had lacked before: it is no denigration to claim for Du Bois the title of chief publicist of the movement. When Pan-Africanism was hardly more than a dream, his vision of its possibilities was compelling and strong, even though as time passed he could not fill in the spaces of his dream with clear details.

When he came to the editorship of *The Crisis* in 1910 Du Bois made the magazine "a valuable source of Pan-African ideas."[3] By 1919 he was concerned enough with the subject and influential enough with the NAACP to persuade them to support a second Pan-African congress (considered the first by some historians) in Paris, the first congress he organized. This meeting, though lacking participation sufficiently broad (especially African) and official to qualify as a truly representative congress, was bigger and more specific about its Pan-African aspirations than the first relatively tentative though groundbreaking convocation had been. Its fifty-seven delegates (sixteen from the United States, more than the number from any other country) did not, as Legum pointed out, declare the right of colonized African states to absolute independence but called for the lesser right of these states "to participate" in their own governance "as fast as their development permits." The black representatives convened in 1919 also stated the "need for international laws to protect the natives," for laws to prevent "exploitation by foreign capital," to end slavery and capital punishment, and the right of native Africans to a good education.

The third congress in 1921 which met symbolically enough at both London and Brussels, revealed a split between the aims of the

Franco-African Blaise Diagne and his followers and the more radical Du Bois, over the direction of the still nascent movement. Diagne, a Senegalese deputy in the French National Assembly, had been French commissioner general in World War I and was at least as well known a spokesman internationally as Du Bois. He had previously used his influence as a member of the French Assembly (for unlike the English—and one might almost say the Americans—the French sought to incorporate colonials into their political system) to enable the shaky 1919 congress to meet in Paris when pressures from Western bloc nations would not permit its opening elsewhere. Though he denied neither his allegiance to other Africans or blacks, Diagne was a product of the French assimilationist colonial system and said he thought of himself as a Frenchman first. Therefore, he would not sign what he considered an excessively aggressive "Declaration to the World," sometimes called the "London Manifesto."

The breach between the two leaders was smoothed over if not completely healed by the meeting's end, but clearly the 1923 and 1927 congresses, the former in London and Lisbon and the latter in New York, showed that the movement's first period of fruitfulness was over, and probably new conditions would have to come into existence for it to grow vigorously again. As J. Ayodele Langley noted in *Pan-Africanism and Nationalism in West Africa, 1900–1945*, the West African response to this first phase of what would become a movement demanding absolute autonomy for African states, a phase dominated though by no means exclusively determined by black New World intellectuals such as Du Bois, was "a mixture of enthusiasm, mild criticism, and an attitude which implied that there was no direct *rapport* between Du Bois's Pan-Africanism and the new Pan-West African nationalism."[4]

Throughout the 1920s also, the movement was disturbed and confused by what seemed the ideological split between Du Bois and Marcus Garvey. This disjuncture within the movement is difficult to trace because both Du Bois and Garvey were rather fuzzy about specific plans for the future Africa that existed in their imaginations. Du Bois appeared to favor an Africa operating on a more industrialized basis under some sort of democratic, socialistic system, with much of the necessary expertise for running this political entity provided by a black American elite aided somehow by white technological resources. The blueprint for Garvey's "Back to Africa" scheme was no more precise than Du Bois's though its emphasis upon black pride and self-sufficiency made it justifiably popular with many American Negroes. Garvey appeared to stress the migration of socially heterogeneous groups of New World blacks to Africa, where they would engage in capitalistic endeavors as far removed from white interference as possible. While it is not true that Garvey called for the rapid and nearly total depopulation of black areas in the New World as his detractors often asserted, he did carry with him from his early life in the West Indies a sensitivity to skin color as a determinant of character that offended many lighter American Negroes (and some light-skinned leaders such as Du Bois and his colleague at the NAACP, Walter White) whom he did not consider truly black. In the real Africa distant from the occasionally overlapping dreams of Du Bois and Garvey, Garvey's influence upon Pan-Africanists was not as negligible as Du Bois hoped, and it irked him that the two should in any way be linked, as in Du Bois's mind they clearly were not.

Several radical changes in world conditions and in the leadership of the movement would take place before the next phase of Pan-Africanism helped make political independence a reality for most African nations. First, the driving spirit behind the movement shifted from one of its bases in black America to "third-world" West Indian and African regions. Even so, the new leadership—men such as George Padmore, C. L. R. James, Wallace Johnson, Kwame Nkrumah, and Jomo Kenyatta (none of whom were Americans)—recognized, in Padmore's words, that they were building "upon the pioneering work of Du Bois."[5] Second, in the aftermath of the Great Depression and World War II, the old Western colonial powers were weakened and the African states had grown more potent, to the point that the possibility of independence was a strong reality, a practical problem to be solved by insiders rather than a theoretical issue to be envisioned from without. Du Bois convened, though he neither organized nor directed, the first postwar Pan African congress in Manchester, England, in 1945. At this congress for the first time the participants officially issued a "demand for Black African autonomy and independence." The membership was working class oriented to an extent far greater than at any of the earlier congresses, was comprised of far more Africans and far fewer Americans, and was far more aggressive than the prior congresses had been.

Du Bois voiced the feelings of the congress when he announced that while the new African states that must come into being would make mistakes, in part because they had not been given the opportunity to participate meaningfully in their own governance, such errors would be learned from, and were a necessary concomitant of the new powers of self-determination that must come to Africa. The seed of independence that he helped plant early in the century ultimately produced a sturdy growth as he had dreamed it would in 1900, though not one necessarily in the precise form of his dream. Forces and agents of history outside his control and independent of him had worked for its success and guided its maturation, but from the start and all along he provided insight and inspiration.

All these reverberations from his original regard for Africa and Pan-Africanism were many years away in the future, far from the time he spent in Atlanta in the century's first decade. Still, his recognized position in African-American affairs sprang directly from his activities during this period.

As early as 1904 future African leaders such as the Ghanaian nationalist and historian J. E. Casely-Hayford (1886–1930) began corresponding with Du Bois, whose interest in Africa was cultural as well as political. Du Bois's scheme for an *Encyclopedia Africana*, a work he dreamed would cover "the chief points in the history and condition of the Negro Race," began during the Atlanta years also, as his letter of 5 April 1909 to the West African statesman Edward Wilmot Blyden indicates.

Du Bois was never a deep or profound student of African politics or art. His attitude toward the motherland was distinctly idyllic both before, during, and after his first visit to the continent in 1923. He was dead wrong in 1903 that "the central fact of African life, political, social and religious, is its failure to integrate,"[6] for the direct opposite idea—that integration is the chief fact of African life—is a basic element of African existence, or was before modernization that Du Bois knew little about only very recently became another condition of African life. Du Bois was wrong also in 1925 when he claimed that in Africa "the energetic, are the dead. In Africa the 'lazy' survive and live."[7] He never showed much awareness of politics internal to Africa, of the power struggles in Ethiopia and Liberia for example. Africans and Afro-Americans both came to criticize his idea that the "Talented Tenth" of black America could significantly aid African development.

Still his accomplishments in presenting African history to the American world were many, just as his symbolic significance as a Pan-Africanist was important. His emphasis upon the key role the struggle for colonies in Africa played in World War I was a helpful corrective to analyses that ignored the war's imperialistic origins. His insistence that Africa had a rich artistic and social history of which both white and black America should be aware was a necessary and much-needed antidote to the usually absent or hostile account of Africa that most American libraries and school systems presented. His reiterated demand that African nations be granted self-determination was a spur to black and white leaders alike. Though his view of Africa was ever a romantic fable, for many black Americans it was the first or only positive view they would receive, and for others it would stimulate further research.[8] Overall, his interest in Africa was highly salutary.

II   "Booker T. and W. E. B."

The second activity during the Atlanta years that helped define Du Bois's identity as a race leader was his controversial interaction with Booker T. Washington. Early in his career Du Bois had applauded Washington. In September 1895 he sent from Wilberforce, where he had probably met Washington during a speech the educator gave there, a message complimenting him on what would later be called Washington's "Atlanta Compromise" speech: "let me heartily congratulate you upon your phenomenal success in Atlanta—it was a word fitly spoken." Thereafter, Du Bois carried on a lifelong dialogue with Washington and what he considered were Washington's ideas, a dialogue he continued as a monologue after Washington died in 1915. Washington only rarely responded in print, though apparently he said a good deal in private communication. Du Bois's deep concern to find the best road for Negroes to travel on their quest for equality, a journey he knew would be painfully difficult at best, was the primary reason for treating Washington and his social theories to such constant scrutiny. There is also a point at which Du Bois's concern becomes an obsession, however, indicating that his interest in Washington was more than academic. Furthermore, there were always those who for selfish reasons desired to exploit the rift between the two men and hopefully weaken the fragile political resources of the black community. The same kind of mentality tried to cause friction between Malcolm X and Martin Luther King when those men led somewhat separate parties forward in the struggle for black liberation.

The course of Du Bois's disagreement with Washington is too long and complex for full analysis here and only its outlines can be noted. First, it should be remembered that Du Bois usually combined praise with his criticisms of Washington when he discussed him publicly. As early as *The Philadelphia Negro* Du Bois acknowledged that Washington had been unfairly attacked for rightly arguing that trade unions placed many obstacles in the way of Negroes seeking "material advancement." In *The Gift of Black Folk* Du Bois praised Washington's autobiographical *Up From Slavery* and his attempts to "begin . . . an industrial democracy in the South, based upon education." In the *Crisis* for March 1929, Du Bois recollected fondly Washington's method for "remembering" names of people who greeted him when he was on tour: he would first send his secretary into a room to find out who was there, and the secretary would then relay the names of the guests back to the forgetful Washington.

Often Washington reciprocated with praise of Du Bois. Du Bois mentions approvingly in his *Autobiography* that Washington spoke at the 1911 "Atlanta Conference on the Negro Artisan" and commended Du Bois for organizing the series in the "painstaking and systematic manner" that Du Bois always followed on his major projects. Washington had previously sent Du Bois a letter "most heartily and earnestly" commending Du Bois for the 1906 conference on "The Negro Common School."

Du Bois and Washington also shared many views, or held similar views, as a number of critics have noted.[9] Young Du Bois's plea in *The Philadelphia Negro* for "patience" on the part of blacks in their striving for equal opportunity was something Washington could only have agreed with. Du Bois's later interest in the power that could be developed through the accumulation of wealth by Negro laborers is not distant from Washington's emphasis upon the need to train Negroes to perform well at laboring tasks on farms and in factories so that they could acquire the prosperity that would presumably raise them from their lowly position in American society. And Du Bois's controversial idea expressed most vigorously in the 1930s that Negroes should take advantage of the segregation they had been forced into and even exploit it for their own benefits, is not totally dissimilar to Washington's acceptance of segregation as a kind of sociopolitical haven within which Negroes might operate, to their economic and social advantage.

But the occasional praise the men exchanged and the similarities in their thinking should not obscure the very deep ideological and personal antagonism Du Bois felt toward Washington. In his *Autobiography* Du Bois recollected the "bitter" controversy with Washington even while maintaining that their theories of black progress were not absolutely contradictory. Du Bois suggests that a basic cause for their disagreement was his own belief in the need to educate that "Talented Tenth" of Negroes "who through their knowledge of modern culture could guide the American Negro into a higher civilization." Washington, Du Bois claimed, minimized the importance of higher education for blacks and "discouraged philanthropic support" of it. Du Bois also felt that the vocational training given blacks within Washington's plan was unsound in an increasingly complicated and technologically advanced world, that Washington was preparing workers who could compete only for the very lowest kinds of jobs because they lacked skill in trades. Du Bois also very passionately objected to what he considered Washington's posture of meek conciliation to whites in the matter of civil rights. To Du Bois, acceptance of anything less than complete political and social equality would mean race suicide.

Du Bois also vigorously objected to what he termed "the Tuskegee Machine" directed by Washington, a network of black newspapers, educational institutions, and relationships with white political entrepreneurs. Du Bois contended that the machine gave Washington some power as a black but also permitted greater manipulation of Negroes. Du Bois especially opposed what he felt were Washington's systematic efforts to suppress opposition to himself as a leader from within the black community. Time and again Du Bois found that money for projects Washington considered inimical to his interests were not funded or were underfunded. And as early as 1903 he found occasion to object to Washington's overreaction to criticism, when Washington or his supporters had the feisty but deeply committed Negro activist Monroe Trotter jailed for heckling a Boston speech of Washington's. Du Bois did not advocate Trotter's violent verbal attack and criticized him for it, but he more emphatically disagreed with Washington's dangerously intimidating response.

Charting Du Bois's attitude toward Washington is complicated by occasional shifts in Du Bois's political positions during his long career. On the surface Washington was more consistent, but as his most sympathetic and understanding contemporary biographer, Louis Harlan, says of him in *Booker T. Washington, The Making of a Black Leader, 1856–1901,* Washington "was forced from childhood to deceive, to simulate, to wear the mask. With each subgroup of blacks or whites that he confronted, he learned to play a different role." Often Washington's ultimate plans for blacks were "deeply hidden" beneath the masks he donned at will in public, permitting him to preach separateness but covertly to "attack . . . the racial settlement he publicly accepted," like a double agent who infiltrated the white power elite in order to subvert it—a Br'er Rabbit.

Du Bois continued to be alternately and sometimes concurrently sympathetic and harsh toward Washington until he himself died. While his fictionalized account of Washington's last years and his weird death in *The Ordeal of Mansart* (1957) were as unnecessary to that work as they were virulent, his final remark about the basic conflict between himself and Washington, as reported by Leslie Lacy, is revealing and sympathetic. Du Bois said that Washington, born into slavery in the South, had "felt the lash," and that he, Du Bois, had not. Du Bois was typically astute here. Washington as a boy and young man was awed by whites and had seen grown black men whipped. Du Bois was clearly intellectually superior to his white classmates, and his first sharply unpleasant awareness of his race came when a little girl refused his calling card. Personality differences undoubtedly contributed to the dispute: Washington seemed so much more friendly and outgoing, and appeared to be more at home with different groups, though one suspects at heart he was not; Du Bois, in contrast, had far greater self-confidence though he was sometimes more openly ill at ease. Possibly toward the older and more established man Du Bois felt a certain ambivalence—such as a son might feel toward a father who had rejected him—seeing in Washington an authority figure who should give him guidance and recognition, but whom he would ultimately have to reject to establish himself.

III *Fighting for Equality*

The third area of nonacademic activity Du Bois engaged in during his Atlanta years was his attempt to found an organization that would demand civil rights for blacks. This attempt resulted in

part from Du Bois's and others' feelings that the conciliatory
Washington should not be allowed to represent the race in its fight
for freedom, but chiefly from Du Bois's awareness of the cruelly
inferior situation of the race in America. In Atlanta he saw in
operation Jim Crow laws that daily segregated Negroes in housing
and education and disqualified them from most good jobs. He saw
too what horrifying depths race hatred could sink to. The most
traumatic instances of this murderous bigotry were the killing and
dismemberment of Sam Hose in 1899 by a white mob, some of
whom later exhibited his knuckles in a grocery store window on
Mitchell Street in Atlanta, and what Julius Lester called the
"Atlanta pogrom" of 1906, which resulted in the deaths of at least
four blacks.

Du Bois wrote his famous "A Litany At Atlanta" on the way
back to the city to protect his family during this pogrom. He also
bought and intended to use a gun if he or his family were
attacked. But he knew that neither poems nor individual defiance
would solve the Negro's awful predicament, and sought the
creation of some organization that could offer more substantial
and sustained protest. His wish culminated in the Niagara Movement, which from its inception in 1905 until its death (or its
assimilation into the larger and better financed National Association for the Advancement of Colored People) advocated freedom
of speech and criticism for blacks, enfranchisement for black
males, abolition of all caste distinctions based upon race or color,
the right to the best education possible regardless of class or race,
and insisted that laws be enforced in the same fashion upon the
rich as well as upon the poor. The organization was militant but
nonviolent, and its members were black men from the "Talented
Tenth" from whom Du Bois expected so much. The group grew
slightly from the twenty-nine men who attended the first meeting
on 9 July 1905 on the Canadian soil of Fort Erie just outside
Buffalo, New York. They met thereafter in 1906 at Harper's Ferry,
West Virginia, in Boston in 1907, and in Oberlin, Ohio, in 1908.
Never a mass movement with great support, the organization, as
Henry Lee Moon pointed out in *The Emerging Thought of W. E.
B. Du Bois*, "demonstrated the need for the possibilities of a
militant organization to advance the cause of black folk in
America." Du Bois was always proud of his work with the Niagara
Movement.

Clearly the Atlanta years were highly productive for Du Bois. At the same time he came to realize there that his original plans for the Atlanta conferences could not be realized partly because of his own increasing visibility and notoriety. His marriage, he confided in his *Autobiography*, though "not an absolutely ideal union" was, he steadfastly maintained, "happier than most," but he felt that his "main work was out in the world" and not at home, which was where his wife functioned best. And the death of their son "tore our lives in two." The "city's careless sewage" caused the death, but his wife, he would later claim to Shirley Graham, "never forgave God for the unhealable wound." Nor would she forgive her husband. After the death their lives together were even more reserved.

He was also discovering that "he could not be a calm, cool, and detached scientist while Negroes were being lynched, murdered, and starved." His life as a social scientist and spokesman for the race during the Atlanta years brought him many successes and a few failures, a few feelings of dissatisfaction with his inability to get closer to the high goals he had set for himself and his race. He was at another dead end—though one which could have been attractive to a lesser man—and ready for a change. The form that change would take was determined by the newly formed NAACP, which removed Du Bois from his primary role in life as an academic social scientist in the South and directed him toward a new career as a crusading journalist and as a "master of propaganda" for his race. That removal, however, would probably never have occurred save for a book which more than any other single factor made Du Bois famous in and outside America.

IV   The Souls of Black Folk: *The Man Behind the Veil*

Life in America in 1903 was in some ways the same as it had always been: in 1902 the East had been ripped by anthracite coal mining strikes caused by low wages, lockouts, and vicious working conditions which one management representative claimed that God had ordained the mine owners to control. Americans were still reading Thomas Dixon's most powerfully and viciously racist novel *The Leopard's Spots* (1902). But there was also a fresh and critical spirit abroad in the fat land. Jacob Riis's *The Battle With the Slums* and Ida M. Tarbell's *History of the Standard Oil Company* tilted with urban, corporate forces whose growth was bringing such great power and prosperity and social pestilence to the American way of life. In 1903 the Ford Motor Company was formed, the Wright brothers made their first flights over the quiet sand-dunes at Kitty Hawk, and what would later be called Panama was nudged into rebellion from Columbia—all events whose beat quickened America's energetic march into the twentieth century.

Also in 1903 Du Bois published *The Souls of Black Folk*, his best known and most widely read and respected work, a collection of essays that provided an impetus to his life work and to black history which ensured that neither would be quite the same afterward. For in writing about black souls and his own, Du Bois transformed himself into a race leader who with both passion and scholarship revealed with shrewdness, honesty, and artistic sophistication a level of black existence that had never been shown before. Further, the book demonstrated for all time that black invisibility resulted from white disregard or blindness and not from black insubstantiality.

Du Bois revised for the book a number of essays he had previously published in magazines, arranged them in an order he determined for artistic purposes, added transitional passages, and most significantly added one new essay (which in fact brought together a number of vagrant ideas and phrases from remarks he had made in speeches and written previously) which he called "Of Mr. Booker T. Washington and Others." Through his reworking, rearranging, and creation of materials, *The Souls of Black Folk* became a coherent and skillfully constructed book and not simply a collection of old essays. The unity the work exhibits results partly from its formulation at various times by a mind highly unified in its concern, but partly from a conscious, artistic plan.

Some of the reasons for the book's unparalleled impact upon a diversity of readers are obvious, others seem almost to defy analysis, to be rooted deeply in the tangled personality of Du Bois himself and how he projected parts of his character and life into his work—parts but not the whole, for the book at once reveals and conceals, as though he had drawn a penciled image of himself and erased some of his sharpest features, lending a clearer but not necessarily more precise impression of himself to the lines that remained.

It was Du Bois's personality as it emerged through the pages of his book, the inner life and being of the man, that so commanded the attention of his readers. Now calm, now lyrical, now bitter and highly ironic, always seeming to talk to individual readers yet to talk with some distance between him and them—or with a veil between them not unlike the veil of color he refers to in many of his essays—Du Bois is always personally narrating experiences or presenting facts and statistics. He appears before the reader as a live, engaged, involved speaker, not an intimate friend necessarily but a human being willing occasionally to reveal intimate details, always in command of what he wants his individual readers to know and how he wants them to feel. There was, of course, an inherent fascination and tragedy in the material that he communicated to his audience, the inherent drama of the black experience. Yet to the telling of this drama he brought the skills of an artist, orchestrating the previously published material together with fresh material into a coherent and new entity.

Du Bois began *The Souls of Black Folk* with a "Forethought," an invocation to the "Gentle Reader" that "herein lie buried many things which if read with patience may show the strange meaning of being black here at the dawning of the Twentieth Century." His voice is quiet, even apologetic and understated as he continues to suggest that "this meaning is not without interest to you, Gentle Reader; for the problem of the Twentieth Century is the problem of the color line." He further entreats the reader, beseeching "I pray you, then, receive my little book in all charity, studying my words with me, forgiving mistake and foible for the sake of the faith and passion that is in me, and seeking the grain of truth hidden there."

His statement that "the problem of the Twentieth Century is the problem of the color line" has often been quoted, but generally out of the richly ironic context in which Du Bois embedded it. Here at his book's outset he is all courtesy and almost meekness, as he modestly introduces the devastating fact that racial prejudice is the chief problem of modern times. Of course all contemporary times are modern times to the people living in them, but Du Bois was writing at the start of the century, a time when naturally an era's modernity would be emphasized. The gentleness of his tone, the hesitancy with which he offers what is really a bitter denunciation of the modern world—and he continues humbly to explain that he seeks only "to sketch in vague, uncertain outline, the spiritual world in which ten thousand thousand Americans live and strive"—are parts of Du Bois's rhetorical strategy of persuasion. Not exactly a mask behind which the real spokesman for black rights stands hidden, Du Bois's literary style here is a device to enable him to control and channel what must have been his fury at the role he and other black Americans were forced to play in American society.

In his first two major works he employed established academic forms, but in *The Souls of Black Folk* he really created his own form. He created a kind of autobiography but not always of himself. He used himself as a representative figure sometimes, but more often he wrote of others of his race who were victims of white society. He wrote an autobiography of his race, occasionally illustrating conditions by personal anecdote, or by more generalized historical narrative. Often he used statistical data to provide insights into the life of the race much as a biographer would supply details of daily existence to fill in some area of his subject's life story. But what he wrote about himself, and what he wrote about his race, each reflected upon the other, generating and regenerating a bright light illuminating both self and race.

He needed a single perspective from which to relate all the varied information he presented, so that his remarks would not seem random and disorganized and thereby lose impact. Always a man of many skills and interests, a danger all his life was that he could become fragmented, but he never did because he seemed capable of tying together nearly everything in his life. The same is true of the persona he seems to have unthinkingly created to deliver his message in *The Souls of Black Folk*. That person who declares and documents the need for justice to black Americans is and is not Du Bois just as the Benjamin Franklin written about in Franklin's *Memoirs* is and is not Franklin, and the "he" of *The Autobiography of Henry Adams* is and is not Adams. In all three of these American autobiographies (or in Frederick Douglass's works about himself) there is a strong resemblance between the real man who writes the book and the presumably real man who is written about, but in all the works there is also an artist's hand at the job, constructing an image for the public to view.

Part of Du Bois's image as it emerges through the pages of the book is that he is a very polite, reasonable, courteous, sometimes dreamily poetic chap. But what his words say underneath their veneer of calm reflection is as shocking as anything the muckrakers of his day were depicting in their generally more direct and journalistic style, for his language, whether he is engaged in "fine writing" or nostalgic reminiscence of his early days in the South or delivering a relatively bald recital of census reports and school attendance figures, presents terrible truths. Sometimes he seems verbose, as when he writes about "ten thousand thousand Americans" instead of ten million who are black and striving in the land, or when he writes "the weary Emancipator passed to his rest" instead of "Lincoln died." But he knows that ten thousand thousand is a far weightier mass than ten million, and he knows best how to dramatize the painful ordeal not the real politician, Lincoln, but what the real politician Lincoln had become to the freed slaves, had endured, and how to suggest that this mythic Lincoln might have found a relief in death. Du Bois's seemingly orotund prose in these and other passages then not only contributes to creating a single voice that permits him to tell his tale with a restraint that lends power to his narrative, but also to compress meaning into his phrases.

In writing about black souls and about himself, Du Bois developed a number of connected themes. Chief among these are the special difficulty blacks have living in America, the contributions black Americans have made to American history and culture, the attempts of black people to rise above the prejudices that have so unfairly denied them equality in America, and how individuals and the race might best achieve equality. But Du Bois was not a black nationalist in *The Souls of Black Folk*. He prefaced a poem and a bar of music to the start of his first chapter, "Our Spiritual Strivings," a practice he follows in each successive chapter. The poem is by the British poet Arthur Symons and tells of a person crying out in despair for a kind of life which he will apparently never be able to achieve. The music is a bar from one of what Du Bois termed the "sorrow songs," the Negro spiritual "Nobody Knows the Trouble I've Seen." The white poet's name is supplied in the text, but the spirituals that introduce each chapter are unnamed until the book's conclusion. In the first chapter and most of the succeeding chapters, a black work of art exists side by side with a white. Unless the reader knows black music he or she will not recognize the allusion to black music, however, until the end of the book, a subtle way of underscoring black invisibility even while connecting the two races in their strivings. In this first chapter, while both works of art speak of despair, the black

artifact provides some limited suggestion of hope in its reference to
Jesus Christ.

The chapter itself focuses on a question the entire book attempts
to answer, and for which many answers but no one, final answer
will be given: "How does it feel to be a problem?" How does it feel
to be black? The question is asked by someone from the other,
white world, and is asked with no awareness of its intrusiveness
nor of the pain it brings to the one who is asked. The narrating "I"
of the chapter treats the question at first almost playfully. "I smile,
or reduce the boiling to a simmer, as the occasion may require."
There is nothing threatening or direct in his response to the
question, for immediately the narrator begins recollecting his
earliest years, his "days of rollicking boyhood . . . where the dark
Housatonic" flowed between mountains into the sea. He remembers that it was in "a wee wooden schoolhouse," perhaps the last
place anyone would expect to learn a fact that would control one's
life and destiny, "that the revelation first burst . . . upon" him,
"when the shadow swept across me." The occasion was innocent
enough, nothing dangerous it would appear, for it involved the
refusal of a new girl to accept his calling-card. So a simple event
introduced the traumatic fact into his life that he was forever
different from his white schoolmates, and revealed to him his
place behind the "veil."

What must have been (whether or not it occurred in precisely
this way) a shocking event in Du Bois's life, or rather in the life of
the narrator who is recollecting his past in this chapter, is revealed
very simply, without much explanation or elaboration. On the
surface Du Bois presents his response as one of calm deliberation,
but one senses this masks what could only have been an excru-
ciatingly humiliating experience, since it involved his rejection for
being different, a painful experience for any adolescent. Du Bois
then leads from this personal episode and its lesson into a broadly
philosophic generalization about the stigmatized predicament of
all black Americans, using a technique constant throughout his
text, following a short personal passage with a general commentary and then with passages reinforcing his point by advancing
historical or sociological data.

In this instance his memory of childhood becomes an event
illustrating racial history. "After the Egyption and Indian, the
Greek and Roman, the Teuton and Mongolian, the Negro is a sort
of seventh son, born with a veil, and gifted with second-sight in

this American world . . . which . . . only lets him see himself through the revelation of the other," the white world. Here Du Bois is careful to link a special gift ("second-sight") with a restriction, so that terrible as it is, the stigma of blackness contains positive elements, a magical and compensatory specialness reinforced by the ambivalence suggested by the veil Negroes are born with. Then Du Bois enters upon one of the most famous paragraphs in American literary history, concluding that Negroes in America must look at themselves "through the eyes of others . . . measuring" their souls "by the tape of a world that looks on in contempt and pity," creating within the black American a feeling of "twoness,—an American, a Negro; two souls, two thoughts, two unreconciled strivings . . . in one dark body, whose dogged strength alone keeps it from being torn asunder."

The incisive thrust and high velocity of Du Bois's sudden attack here—not an attack on anyone directly or named—is made more effective by being placed after his courteous, ironic start and his dreamy recollection of childhood prejudice. Though his language is still relatively reserved (relative to the agonizing experience he is describing) he has lifted his prose beyond the level of nostalgic reminiscence or philosophic musing, so that he can write vigorous phrases such as "unreconciled strivings," "two warring ideals," "dogged strength," and "torn asunder." He then combines understatement with some strong and unacademic language to state another major idea of the chapter, that the American Negro does not want to Africanize America or "bleach his Negro soul in a flood of white Americanism. . . . He simply wishes to make it possible for a man to be a Negro and an American, without being cursed and spit upon by his fellows, without having the doors of Opportunity closed roughly in his face." The word "simply" reinforces how modest are the black American's desires, how civilized and reasonable his request. The words "cursed and spit upon" underscore the enormity of the crime against black people, and suggest that while the problem may be simple, the solution will not. The words also suggest the Christliness of the Negro's scorned life.

Chapter 2, "Of the Dawn of Freedom," was one of Du Bois's favorite pieces of writing. He begins it with another phrase that has since become famous—"The problem of the Twentieth Century is the problem of the color line"—which thrusts upon an international level the national and personal problem he had just discussed so eloquently. "On the Dawn of Freedom" investigates historically the same dilemmas that Du Bois described from the perspective of personal and group psychology in chapter 1, and examines essentially "the period of history from 1861 to 1872 so far as it relates to the American Negro" and in a subtle fashion to himself. Du Bois does not write of his own person in the chapter which features "an account of that government of men called the Freedmen's Bureau," though through his life he would be personally, highly involved with explaining what really happened to American Negroes when for the first time as a community they were given their supposed freedom.

He retells impressionistically and with a dignified beauty how many slaves left their homes in the South to find liberation at the camps of invading Northerners, and with passion relates the heroic, badly supported, and ultimately tragic endeavor to maintain the Freedmen's Bureau, an institution supported by the hopes and bodies of thousands of ex-slaves, and usually led by a few white military men who tried to cope with the chaos wrought by the impact of an ill-prepared emancipation upon a nation of blacks whose culture had been rooted in forced servitude for centuries. He focuses especially upon "the freed slave, bewildered between friend and foe," living in a land still hostile to him, who "shrank from the master who still strove for their chains" and "fled to the friends that had freed them, even though those friends stood ready to use them as a club for driving the recalcitrant South back into loyalty." He concludes that the "hastily organized Bureau" which ultimately became a full-fledged government of men, though far from perfect, accomplished more than it should have been expected to, considering the conditions it was forced to operate under—adverse political conditions and social prejudices and shady business practices far more engrained in the American scene than it was. It blundered and allowed frauds committed in its name, but under the leadership of men such as Major-General Oliver O. Howard, it accomplished much, its greatest success being "the planting of the free school among Negroes." Here Du Bois underscored one of the recurring themes in his book and in his work as a whole, the absolute necessity for Negro education, calling especial attention to what he called "the crusade of the New England schoolm'm" during the period.

As always he was careful to note all self-initiated attempts by Negroes to improve their conditions. Particularly poignant was the "remarkable start in the development of thrift" that black Americans made when they placed their hard-earned cash into the Freedmen's Bank, an institution Du Bois says was "morally and practically" though not legally connected to the Freedmen's Bureau. The bank failed through largely white mismanagement and fraud, destroying the savings of those who had so hopefully brought their meager savings to it.

While Du Bois was a revisionist historian through most of *Souls of Black Folk*, for example, in his partial exculpation of the Freedmen's Bureau, he was still a relatively conservative social theorist on many issues. In discussing the problem of Negro enfranchisement he still held that "every sensible man, black and white, would easily have chosen . . . restricted Negro Suffrage" following emancipation. The book's next chapter, however, so innocently and deceptively titled "Of Mr. Booker T. Washington and Others," makes him appear more radical. In chapter 2 Du Bois concerned himself with a movement of men. In chapter 3 he limited himself to a man who was practically a movement.

The conflict between Du Bois and Washington and their respective adherents has had a long and torturous history. Since Du Bois was addressing himself in *The Souls of Black Folk* to the best ways to ensure black survival and advancement—having in chapter 2 just noted the failure of the Freedmen's Bureau to achieve either—it was only natural for him to turn to the black man in his own time whose program for each was perhaps the best known in the country. Thus, Du Bois was not at this stage of his book or his career going out of his way to subject Washington to critical scrutiny.

On the surface the essay seems a balanced appraisal of Washington's virtues and defects as a race leader. It begins by emphasizing Du Bois's respect for Washington's accomplishments. But under its surface the essay is filled with irony that constantly withdraws with one hand what it seems to be offering as praise with the other. At the time of its original appearance many missed this irony, reading the essay only as a diatribe against Washington, who was not usually openly criticized, and who was almost as much as his white namesake, a monumental figure of admiration (to liberal whites anyway). Du Bois's irony is clear from the start—in, for example, his choice of an epigraph to the chapter, a fragment from Byron calling for militance to end the life of "unmanned" slavery. Washington is viewed throughout the essay as a compromiser, one who was willing to accept social and political subservience in return for the chance that Negroes might achieve the vocational training he felt, according to Du Bois's redaction of Washington's ideas, would make them economically secure. In Washington's Atlanta speech, which Du Bois terms "by all odds the most notable thing in Mr. Washington's career," Washington declared that "in all things purely social we can be as separate as the five fingers, and yet one as the hand in all things essential to mutual progress." Du Bois attacks this view of progress by holding that the concept is destructive to black manhood and politically naive. But he does so at first cautiously. He constantly refers to his subject politely as "Mr. Booker T. Washington" or "Mr. Washington," at the same time neglecting to use the honorific "Doctor" which so many affected in referring to the founder of Tuskeegee.

Much of what seems praise at the essay's start disguises latent scorn. For example, Du Bois claims that Washington's Atlanta speech, the beauty of which was according to Du Bois that both the radical racist and politically conservative Southerner could think that it advanced their views, has turned Washington into "certainly the most distinguished Southerner since Jefferson Davis," for whom Du Bois had utter contempt. Commending Washington for his "singleness of vision and thorough oneness with his age," Du Bois adds quietly, "It is as though Nature must needs make men narrow in order to give them force." Du Bois's direct criticisms are offered with seeming diffidence: "One hesitates . . . to criticize a life which, beginning with so little, has done so much."

The bulk of the essay undercuts Washington as a race leader. Du Bois first briefly reviews the history of black leadership in the new world, noting the many often violent attempts such as Nat Turner's rebellion to attain freedom. After what he calls the "Revolution of 1876" and its consequent resuppression of the Negro, Du Bois states that Frederick Douglass emerged as the great advocate of "assimilation *through* self-assertion, and on no other terms." Washington however replaced Douglass, and Du Bois claims that he is essentially a compromiser willing to "surrender . . . civil and political rights . . . for larger chances of economic development." Washington's plan for the Negro, according to Du Bois, "asks that black people give up" political power, civil rights, and the "higher education of Negro youth" to concentrate their "energies on industrial education, the accumulation of wealth, and the conciliation of the South." This trade has resulted in "disfranchisement of the Negro," legally guaranteed social and civil inferiority, and "withdrawal of aid from institutions for the higher training of the Negro." Blacks have gained little and lost nearly everything in the exchange. "The way," Du Bois says after reviewing the failure of Washington's program, "for a people to gain their reasonable rights is not by voluntarily throwing them away."

As his denunciation of Washington's policies proceeds, Du Bois uses less and less of the quiet, urbane language of his essay's start, and more and more dynamic though still controlled phrasing. In his last paragraph he adopts the orator's tone of solemn restraint under pressure. "The black men of America have a duty to perform, a duty stern and delicate," to oppose Mr. Washington when he is wrong—to glory "in the strength of this Joshua called of God" when he is right, but to "firmly oppose him" when he "apologizes for injustice" or undervalues "the privilege and duty of voting, belittles the emasculating effects of caste discriminations, and opposes the higher training and ambition of our brighter minds." Key words here are the twice-repeated term "duty," which turns opposition to Washington into a positive obligation, and the word "emasculating," which returns to the suggestion implicit in the poem that began Du Bois's essay, that Washington's compromise is destructive to black manhood. In a final, masterful touch, Du Bois listed at his essay's end the rights denied black Americans in his day by invoking the Declaration of Independence, which becomes a document reserved for white Americans, containing rights that will never be attained by blacks through following Mr. Booker T. Washington. That Du Bois's appraisal of Washington's aims and methods is totally accurate and complete is questionable; the total success of his onslaught against the idea of compromise is unquestionable.

"Of the Meaning of Progress," the chapter that follows Du Bois's rhetorical tour de force against Washington, is an unargumentative, relatively light chapter, muted and nostalgic in tone, silent and sad after the powerful polemic that preceded it. The chapter contains an often charming and melancholic remembrance of Du Bois's early days teaching in the Tennessee hills so intellectually distant from Fisk, beyond another kind of veil, a cultural one. As though he were presenting a fairy tale, Du Bois begins this chapter with the traditional "once upon a time" that emphasizes how long ago in his life the events which he is about to narrate took place, during an age when he was "young and happy . . . that summer, seventeen years ago." His storytelling is convincing, and one would never guess from what he writes of his adventures that in reality, they were often quite unpleasant and shocking, such as the here unmentioned rape he experienced with himself as victim. Instead, we meet mainly pleasant and always poor Negroes: thin, homely Josie "with a dark-brown face and thick, hard hair," 'Thenie, "jolly, ugly, goodhearted," or 'Tildy, "a midnight beauty, with starry eyes and tapering limbs." His life is described in a rarely harsh, slightly dim light, like the tones of an old photograph, the light of his dream of youth.

So the mood and pace of "On the Meaning of Progress" is totally unlike that of "Of Mr. Booker T. Washington and Others." The former is highly personal and even romantic in tone, autumnal in mood, while the latter is a fresh, cutting, highly political piece. Both, however, concern black education and neither lets the reader forget that a black man rightly obsessed with racial problems is writing them. "On the Meaning of Progress" tells a story introduced by the lightest of images, describing Du Bois riding to the house of the local commissioner of education with "a pleasant young white fellow" while "the sun laughed and the [river] water jingled." The commissioner invites both men to dinner and offers both men jobs, one in the white school and one in the black. Du Bois ends the story by saying without comment simply "they ate first, then I—alone": almost unconscious racism is simply reported. Du Bois also describes in the essay his return to the region a decade later. The sunniness of the early time is gone, and he meets lives ruined because of their blackness. "In that little valley was a strange stillness as I rode up; for death and marriage had stolen youth and left age and childhood there." While "Of Mr. Booker T. Washington and Others" ended assertively and optimistically, "On the Meaning of Progress" concludes sadly, with Du Bois riding the train back to Nashville "in the Jim Crow car." The essay on "progress" as well as the essay on Washington possesses irony.

In chapter 7 Du Bois asks the reader to ride the Jim Crow car with him again through the black belt of that region. It is again hot in July around Albany, Georgia, where cotton still is king. But while the white aristocrats prosper from the gathering of the crop, black life shows neglect only, depression, "silence . . . and ashes, and tangled weeds." Du Bois describes the kind of depleted, dessicated scene T. S. Eliot would later label as the waste land, modern-day deserted villages where in Du Bois's words, "the buildings were rotten, the bricks were falling out, the mills were silent, and the stores were closed." Here and frequently toward the final half of his book Du Bois confronts directly the race prejudice that had so tainted the education and chance for prosperity of black Americans. He discusses in chapter 9 the apartheid practiced in southern towns, the separateness with which black and white dwellings isolate their inhabitants from each other. Slavery, he claims in a momentary burst of elitism, was sometimes better for both white and black for then at least "one found the best of both races in close contact and sympathy" whereas now the best whites and Negroes never live in close proximity and both "see only the worst of each other."

Even more destructive to the democratic ideal is the fact so obvious to Du Bois, that in the South the mass of blacks is under the domination of the mass of whites. This results in a double code of justice that is most unfair to the blacks, in unequal economic opportunities, and in a pitiable black school system which paid out in Georgia, for example, four dollars to white schools for every one dollar to black. Du Bois then admits in a remark that might surprise readers today who know him primarily as a staunch radical "that it is possible, and sometimes best, that a partially undeveloped people should be ruled by the best of their stronger and better neighbors for their own good" until they can fight their battles alone. But, he says, "the best opinion of the South today is not the ruling opinion." Here again, he says, slavery held certain advantages, for it at least occasionally permitted a "finer sympathy and love between some masters and house servants" which by his day no longer existed.

According to Du Bois the solution to the oppressed condition of the blacks was not to cultivate an alliance with sympathetic whites—though their aid could help. The solution lay instead with the blacks themselves, and with the strength that education and the ability to use the ballot wisely gave them. "Only by a union of intelligence and sympathy across the color-line . . . shall justice and right triumph," he states, but it is clear that he felt blacks would have to get control of their own destiny to make the union efficacious.

Chapter 10 returns more directly to an exploration of the "souls" of black people. "Of the Faith of the Fathers" stresses the role of black religion in providing a reservoir for some few survivals from black African existence, for maintaining some social security amid the disintegrative forces of slavery, and for enabling masses of Negroes to survive in slavery with their humanity intact. Du Bois's skepticism about all institutional religion, black or white, also finds a place in the essay, however, for he asserts that now masses of Negroes are active in churches that seem irrelevant to the spiritual needs of blacks, offering them instead a haven for fashion and amusement.

The almost rambling generalities of "The Faith of the Fathers" are followed by "Of the Passing of the First-Born," a short and uniquely personal chapter telling of Du Bois's son Burghardt's death at three years. Du Bois's life and career were filled with ironies and contradictions, not the least of which was that although much of his writing was autobiographical in some way, there is a part of him very close inside himself that he almost never revealed to the outside world, a love and affection for people and for life that even when he expressed his passions do not seem truly part of him. In "The Passing of the First-Born" his dual drives to reveal and conceal are apparent in the highly literary, formal, sometimes stilted, and yet intensely feeling prose that he employs to describe his beloved son's death: "A perfect life was his, all joy and love, with tears to make it brighter,—sweet as a summer's day. . . . Blithe was the morning of his burial. . . . He knew no color-line . . . the Veil, though it shadowed him, had not yet darkened half his sun."

Du Bois changed his pace quickly in the next chapter, leaving his brief, personal elegy to return to the historical approach he uses often in *The Souls of Black Folk*, to tell about another Negro boy, one who overcame the cruel obstacles placed in his way by the supposedly Christian world of his church, to become a priest great in moral accomplishment if not famous in the land of his birth. "Of Alexander Crummel" is an uplifting hagiography chronicling the life of one of Du Bois's heroes, a man before whom young Du Bois had "bowed . . . instinctively . . . as one bows before the prophets." Crummel's story is an exemplary tale that appears in the text at a crucial moment, after stories narrating death and defeat. Crummel never admitted defeat though the white world, especially his own Episcopal Church, blocked his aspirations whenever it could. The language Du Bois employs is noticeably and suitably inspirational: "out of the temptation of Hate, and burned by the fire of Despair, triumphant over Doubt, and steeled by Sacrifice against Humiliation, he turned at last home across the waters, humble and strong, gentle and determined." To balance out the capitalized abstractions Du Bois fills Crummel's story with the kind of details that would make all but the most unregenerate readers long to see him triumph. Occasionally there is also astringent wit, satire to offset the homiletic prose, for example, when he writes of one racist church official named "Bishop Onderdonk" who "lived at the head of six white steps,—corpulent, red-faced, and the author of several thrilling tracts on Apostolic Succession."

Du Bois knew that although the souls of black folk were experienced in suffering, not all black people would be able to turn the pain into a force driving toward survival and success. The short story "Of the Coming of John" tells of a young Negro man pursued and harried and finally thrust down by the white world around him, who submits to his fate with a strange but not unrealistic combination of stoicism and narcissism. The story is not totally successful as a work of art partly because Du Bois chose to parallel the Negro John's life melodramatically and formulaically with that of a thoroughly reprehensible scoundrel from his home town, a white boy also named John. The Negro John is an idealistic and sensitive young man whose destruction in the South seems assured because it is inevitable that as a teacher of his people he is doomed to clash with the arrogant, paternalistic white judge who is his school supervisor. Although the rape of black women by white men was certainly not uncommon in the South, the scene showing white John's attempted rape of black John's sister seems staged especially to lead to the story's depressing denouement. That white John is also the judge's son seems equally staged.

Artistically deficient, some of the work's political and psychological undercurrents would repay further analysis. When Negro John strikes at his white antagonist to protect his own sister, he is both militant and successful. But then at the story's end he seems ready either to commit a kind of suicide or to enter a state of mystic trance or perhaps both, "his closed eyes toward the Sea" as he senses shadowy whites pursuing him. He meets his fate with a German song on his lips, a detail suggesting his cultural sophistication and definitely not black nationalism. *The Souls of Black Folk*

was written from an integrationist perspective. The life Du Bois's
hero John wants to live contains cultural elements from both black
and white societies. Possibly John's death could be viewed as proof
unconsciously worked out and against Du Bois's surface stance,
that integration was impossible, that blacks must not let themselves be seduced by what appears to be lovely in the white world,
by operas such as Wagner's *Lohengrin*, for example, that John
must leave early in the story because he is black. Whatever John's
death represents, Du Bois's own son would never have to confront
his fate, nor would he be able to achieve Alexander Crummel's.

The latter third of Du Bois's book is filled with death—his son's,
Crummel's, John's. These deaths are not always linked with
despair, but despair is a part of them. The book's concluding
chapter, "Of the Sorrow Songs," is about death and despair but
about hope also, striking an ambivalent ending note. The essay
offers another bit of Negro history written to tell America of a
significant black achievement, the spirituals, "the sole American
music and the most beautiful expression of human experience born
this side of the seas." Du Bois was a pioneer in claiming for these
beautiful songs their rightful recognition as one of the great
contributions of American art to the world. Yet on another level of
his race autobiography he is discussing the message of the spirituals, what they tell of and to black people, the slaves, "the
children of disappointment; they tell of death and suffering and
unvoiced longing toward a truer world." The songs tell of "exile, of
strife and hiding: they grope toward some unseen power and sigh
for rest in the End." They are songs of mothers and children but
not of fathers (remarks the fatherless Du Bois), they are songs of
"rocks and mountains" (remarks the man born in the shadow of
hills) but not songs of home. Communally created and communally performed, they represent a symbol of solidarity and cooperation among black Americans.

But significantly they describe no necrophiliac longings and they
are not songs that accept death. Ultimately, Du Bois claims, they
transcend sorrow. "Through all the sorrow of the Sorrow Songs
there breathes a hope—a faith in the ultimate justice of things."
With artistic craft he placed this chapter last, telling of sorrow and
hope. For though by this time in his life Du Bois had experienced
much of the terrible agony that was a part of black life in America,
he had also experienced much of what was best in that life. And so
his concluding message to America and his final insight into the

souls of black folk presented a dual revelation—showed pain and some slight promise still. The prose of his last paragraphs is assertive and sure. The sorrow songs sing, he says, of despair but often of "triumph and calm confidence" in a faith that one day justice will prevail—in death or in life. He says he does not know if the sorrow songs sing true, but his language suggests that he will live as though the message were true and that justice can be achieved and the racial veil torn. In his book's first paragraph he presented himself as a problem, but his last words look for liberation, and write of sunshine and children singing "Let Us Cheer the Weary Traveller," singing of the traveler who "girds himself, and sets his face toward the Morning, and goes on his way."

V   *The Significance of* The Souls of Black Folk

Compared to Franklin's *Memoirs* or *The Autobiography of Henry Adams, The Souls of Black Folk* offers a much deeper emotional experience for the reader. Compared to James Weldon Johnson's *Along This Way* or Washington's *Up From Slavery* or *The Life and Times of Frederick Douglass*, it is a much more intensely intellectual and historical experience. Ultimately, as with any great book, the sum of its achievement adds up to a total greater than the combination of its parts. Its success is partly due to the way Du Bois leads his readers through various changes—writing now straight history, now personal anecdote, sometimes exhorting, sometimes quietly remembering, occasionally philosophizing. He presents himself in the book as a scholar of facts, a friendly interlocutor, a shrewd analyst of everyday affairs, as he shifts from one role to another with ease. Writing a résumé of the significance of the Freedmen's Bureau that is still a good brief introduction to that subject, or plunging into the depression brought about by his son's death, he is always persuasive, always black, always human and humane. He is at once a solitary Negro American and yet a representative of all Negroes—and an American. His private experiences become prototypical and black history becomes a key to his private life. In *The Souls of Black Folk* nearly every chapter contains both some personal and some more broadly historical drift. In "Of the Sorrow Songs," for example, he tells of the African songs his ancestors passed down from generation to generation and finally sang to him, and he to the world. He then relates that this kind of oral transmission also occurred among the slaves in the South and links African song with himself and with Negro America. The personal detail illuminates history and history provides a context spotlighting personal life.

Urbane and passionate, Du Bois controlled both the voice that narrated each individual essay and the structure that bound all essays together. While his language shifts from the hortatory to the lamentory, from that of the academician to that of the friendly traveler, it always changes purposefully and not merely to demonstrate his stylistic breadth. Certain images reoccur just as certain themes reoccur. Words and phrases about the veil, shadows, clouds, images of doubleness reinforce the picture of repressive Negro life in America, the need for better and higher education, better job opportunities, and the absolute right of American Negroes to total equality. Du Bois's language is usually formal and occasionally portentous or weighty, and sometimes (to the modern reader anyway) pretentiously ornate. But his subject was also high and grave and the language in which he discusses it necessarily sober. Furthermore, part of his strategy was to write as an educated black man, that strange anomaly, to show his white and black audience his command of the native intellectual idiom. Yet he could be trenchant and pointed in his prose, as when he writes "to be a poor man is hard, but to be a poor race in a land of dollars is the very bottom of hardships."

The history of his book's reception is a story in itself. In an introduction to the text Saunders Redding accurately stated that "it is more history making than historical." It was one of those rare books that altered or deeply affected the lives of many who read it, people of various origins and colors. James Weldon Johnson said it had a greater effect on Negro readers than any book written since *Uncle Tom's Cabin*. The black South African writer Peter Abrahams is only one of many Africans who attested to how the book made him for the first time aware of his Negroness. But white readers too have given witness to the book's power and insight, writers as disparate as the German sociologist Max Weber and the Anglo-American novelist Henry James. Perhaps most pleasing to Du Bois, however, were the letters and statements of praise he received from ordinary black and white readers who read the work and were deeply moved by it and who were compelled to communicate their feelings to him, for it was probably these for whom the book was primarily intended and not for professional scholars or civic leaders as were his first two books.[10]

A contemporary of Du Bois, the Negro educator and writer William H. Ferris, wrote of him that "he had no aspiration of becoming a race leader when he wrote his *Souls of Black Folk*."[11] Ferris was wrong, for one of Du Bois's great desires was to become a race leader. *The Souls of Black Folk*, more than any other single publication of Du Bois's, helped him to attain his goal. The book changed his history, and possibly the history of black people in America.

VI John Brown *and the Angry Historian*

Du Bois's next major book, his biography of John Brown (1909), was a distinct departure from his earlier work. On the surface at least not at all autobiographical, *John Brown* was also far less emotionally contained and politically reticent than his first two academically oriented books, and was at the time Du Bois's most uncompromising and combative attack upon the abysmal treatment of blacks in America.

John Brown would remain years after he had written it still very close to him, and he confided once to Herbert Aptheker that it was his "favorite."[12] There was much in the character and story of John Brown that would have appealed to Du Bois above and beyond the fascination he has held for many students of American history. Brown was deeply influenced by the Calvinist tradition as was Du Bois. Both men were stern and yet loving. Brown was a strongly religious man—some would say a religious maniac—and Du Bois's life and writings are pervaded by his spiritual if not his religious fervor. Other biographical similarities could have drawn Du Bois to Brown—witness the passage early in *John Brown* where Du Bois quotes a letter of Brown's wife telling about Brown's pained response to their young daughter's death, which must have reminded Du Bois of his own son's death.

There were more important differences in the lives too. Du Bois was black and an intellectual, and Brown was white and, as Du Bois points out, not "a man of books." Alike in their hatred of slavery, Brown was a man of violent action willing to spill blood in the most gruesome fashion (such as having his enemies hacked to death), whereas Du Bois was publicly almost a pacifist, one who advocated violence reluctantly and only in defensive action. But "A Litany at Atlanta" which he wrote in 1906 reveals the violence of his hatred, and he owned a gun and pledged that he would use it to protect himself and his own. Yet he never retaliated physically against the white society that still, in 1909, held millions of black Americans in virtual slavery. So in writing about Brown he was writing about a man whom he considered a noble American, perhaps too a man who had taken a course of direct action Du Bois unconsciously wished to follow.

The book resulting from Du Bois's close involvement with his subject is often effective in retelling the story of Brown's many personal tragedies and of the single great triumph he achieved through the moral demands he thrust upon the American conscience after his wild sacrifice and military defeat at Harper's Ferry. As a historical work, however, the book is disappointing and ultimately inadequate, certainly compared to the three major works that preceded it.

Throughout his life as a man and scholar with many obligations and few material resources, Du Bois had to compromise to accomplish his objectives. As a scholar, for example, he dealt mainly with secondary rather than with primary sources. His biography of Brown, he explained in a 1907 letter to the civil rights advocate (and fellow biographer of Brown) Oswald Garrison Villard, was to be "an interpretation . . . I am not trying to go very largely to the sources." This led him to perpetuate a number of errors contained in early works on Brown and corrected in later books which he had not seen. Other mistakes he might have rectified had he examined the materials in collections of unpublished materials in New York City, Boston, and elsewhere. Most of his misstatements were minor but their accumulation seriously vitiates the work's scholarly worth, and helps to explain why the book is rarely cited by professional historians.

Du Bois claimed in his preface to *John Brown* that "the only excuse for another life of John Brown is an opportunity to lay new emphasis upon the material which" his many previous biographers had "so carefully collected, and to treat these facts from a different point of view. The view-point adopted in this book is that of the little known but vastly important inner development of the Negro American." Then he admits that "unfortunately, however, few written records of these friendships exist, so that little new material along these lines can be adduced." Therefore, though when possible Du Bois mentions the responses of Frederick Douglass and Martin Delany (the writer and black nationalist) and of the ex-slave Shields Green (who was executed with Brown) to Brown and his scheme, mainly the Negro viewpoint he is expressing in the book in his own rather than those of Brown's black contemporaries.

Nearly all the historical investigation of Brown that Du Bois uses was the work of earlier scholars. He admits this openly and does not offer the ideas of others as his own. Yet it is disappointing to one's concept of Du Bois as a historian, to read page after page of extended quotations from one or another of the four chief sources he lists at the end of his book: Franklin Sanborn, Richard Hinton, James Redpath, and William Connelley. Were the quotations from Sanborn and Redpath omitted or compressed, the book would be significantly briefer.

Du Bois's biography of Brown seems more an extended jeremiad, a polemical attack upon our slave-producing and slavery-sustaining society. "It is not well with this land of ours," he thunders, "poverty is certainly not growing less, wealth is being wantonly wasted, business honesty is far too rare, family integrity is threatened. . . ." Du Bois writes of the corrupt land of his own day that Brown sought to scourge in his. He portrays successfully a mythic, legendary John Brown, though this had been done before at length, for example, by Redpath and Sanborn, and briefly in beautiful talks by Henry David Thoreau and in Herman Melville's poem "The Portent," but beneath the legend his Brown is not always depicted with sufficient historical accuracy.

"John Brown was a stalwart, rough-hewn man," Du Bois writes almost as a praise-singer, "mightily yet tenderly carven. To his making went the stern justice of a Cromwellian 'Ironside,' the freedom-loving fire of a Welsh Celt, and the thrift of a Dutch housewife." He is a figure compounded of elements from an Old Testament prophet, Moses, and Christ, in Du Bois's eyes "the servant and instrument of the almighty," sent, as Brown himself contended, "to deliver Israel out of the hands of the Philistines." His Christliness especially is emphasized. Du Bois uses the fact that he kept sheep as a symbolic detail, titling chapter 4 "The Shepard of the Sheep," and further quotes biblical verses about the angel of the Lord coming upon "country shepards abiding in the field." Brown's words reporting that "the children always come to me" become freighted with Christ-like overtones.

While this view of Brown admirably perceives the moral zeal that was in him, it also separates this zeal from behavorial complications that a historian should examine and that even an impressionistic biographer might want to investigate to prevent his work from being spuriously spiritual. Many parents of Brown's day whipped their children but few kept an account book on the activity as Brown did to record that he had meted to John Brown, Jr. "for disobeying mother, 8 lashes. . . . For telling a lie—8 lashes." He also wrote that one Sunday he whipped this son for one third of his debt, and had John Jr. whip him for the remaining two thirds. Du Bois mentions these details but in no way examines their import. Du Bois relates that at Pottawatomie "John Brown raised his hand and at the signal the victims were hacked to death with broadswords," but fails accurately to investigate the psychological and moral implications of these gruesome and coldly determined killings. In his preface to the edition of 1962, Du Bois noted that Brown's life brought to mind the "bitter debate as to how far force and violence can bring peace and good will." But the debate is virtually absent in his text where it might have found a worthy place had Du Bois written an interpretation of Brown rather than a panegyric upon his high and pure morality.

Although Du Bois's portrait of Brown gains power through simplifying him into a mythic hero, the erasure of fact this poetically conceived image demands harms the book's historic worth. At one point, for example, when explaining how Brown lost much paper profit early in his life, Du Bois attributes the economic crash that crumbled Brown's shaky fortune to Andrew "Jackson's blind tinkering with banking." Whether Jackson's banking policies caused the crash is highly debatable, but that he was not engaged in "blind tinkering" should have been evident to Du Bois who had often demonstrated his awareness of how politics and economics are linked. At other times the messianic pitch of Du Bois's prose leaks into dubiously historical platitudes: "Three lands typified these three things with time planted in the New World: England sent Puritanism, the last flower of the Lutheran revolt; Holland sent the new vigor and thrift of the Renaissance; while Celtic lands and bits of land like France and Ireland and Wales, sent the passionate desire for personal freedom."

Judged by the high standard of his earlier three works and by the standards of history writing contemporary to him, *John Brown* is not a good book.[13] It contains, as usual with Du Bois, patches of good writing. Its view of Brown as a Christ figure is powerfully developed, but at too great length. The book does place greater emphasis upon Brown's relation to black people of his day than did any of Du Bois's sources, but still the imposing figure of Brown dwarfs all else in the book. Du Bois's quotations from earlier works help him construct a massive and compelling view of Brown as a God-inspired scourge of mankind's evil. Perhaps the best portions of the book occur at the very end, when Du Bois and his sources well portray the tragedy of Brown's military defeat and the glory of his spiritual victory. Du Bois's highly wrought writing here seems appropriately matched by Brown's monumental eloquence, and, significantly, while the book's concluding words are Brown's they could just have well been Du Bois's: "You had better—all you people of the South—prepare yourselves for a settlement of this question . . . this question is still to be settled—this Negro question, I mean. The end of that is not yet."[14]

In Du Bois's time the settlement was still coming North and South, and he knew the settlement's working out would be costly in money and lives when it came. But he found in the study of Brown's life a message he wanted Americans to learn: "the cost of liberty is less than the price of repression, even though that cost be blood." Unfortunately, Americans did not always learn the lessons either past history or present books could have taught them. Something else was needed, hopefully something short of blood.

CHAPTER 4

"To Raise My Race"

THE National Association for the Advancement of Colored People evolved from a meeting in New York City in 1909 of white liberals and blacks gathered to discuss a report issued by the white Southerner William English Walling concerning the lynching in 1908 of a black man in Springfield, Illinois. The meeting produced a shaky alliance between the dedicated but sometimes overbearing whites and many of the blacks from Du Bois's Niagara Movement. The Association aimed at becoming a truly national organization of blacks and whites who would attack race prejudice in all its virulent forms. If Negroes were brutalized, if they were not allowed good seats on public conveyances, were forced to attend inferior schools and run-down segregated hospitals, could not enter parks restricted to whites, could not vote, the NAACP aimed at publicizing their plight and combating it through the force of aroused public opinion, the courts, and through federal legislation.

Du Bois came to New York in August 1910 as director of publications and research and editor of *The Crisis*, the official publication of the NAACP. He worked for the organization until 1934, and through his role there and through his books and public talks became probably the best known spokesman for Negro civil rights in America. His tenure as editor and as a member of the board of directors was never easy. He and the other board members had a hard job contending with hostile and dangerous racists all over the country, but they also had to contend with vaguely committed adherents who felt that they were rushing things too fast, and with scoffers who claimed they were not moving fast enough or hard enough against the evils of American bigotry. The leadership had also to contend with each other, with rival egos, and sometimes with the racism of colleagues. Du Bois was sensitive and protectively haughty for a long time, the only black in the inner circle of power where he had to deal with men such as Oswald Garrison Villard (grandson of the abolitionist William Lloyd Garrison) whose Southern wife did not like to meet black people socially in her home. Du Bois claimed in a letter to Mary White Ovington that Villard was "used to advising colored men and giving them orders and . . . simply cannot bring himself to work with one as an equal." But despite all its many difficulties the NAACP stayed together and grew, and Du Bois, generally supported and sustained by friendly fellow workers such as the social worker and socialist Mary White Ovington and the scholar-activist Joel Spingarn, became the Association's chief and best known representative to the American people. He performed as a race leader with pride and energy and sometimes with necessary arrogance tempered by a rarely observed sense of humor: in 1917 he told a cigar company they could use his name for a brand of cigars only "if it isn't too bad."[1] For more than two decades Du Bois edited and wrote tirelessly for *The Crisis*, traveled the world speaking on Negro rights, engaged in seemingly endless controversy both with the white world and the black world he lived in, supported literally hundreds of people and causes that he determined needed his aid, and wrote several books pointing out the glories of the black past and present and harshly attacking the parallel history of black ill-treatment.

He joined the Socialist party in 1910 but resigned in 1912 in what he considered a more pragmatic attempt to gain strength for blacks within the Democratic party. He came to be bitterly disappointed in Woodrow Wilson whom he originally supported as the lesser of evils in 1912, especially when Wilson dramatized his disdain for black interests by practically throwing Monroe Trotter from his office for asking what Wilson termed "impertinent" questions.

Du Bois opposed at first the madness of World War I, seeing it primarily as another squabble among imperialist powers causing the slaughter of the underprivileged for capitalistic profit. But his sympathies came more and more to reside with the French and English, and when America entered the war Wilson had pledged to keep it from, Du Bois declared that blacks had more to gain from involving themselves on what seemed the more just side, than they had in remaining neutral on the grounds that the democracy that was supposedly being fought for was already

denied them by their own country. In July 1918 he issued a call to
"forget our special grievances and close our ranks" in the fight for
world freedom. Julius Lester has called this "perhaps, the
strangest period in W. E. B. Du Bois' long career." Considering,
however, Du Bois's pride in his own New England heritage (one
black ancestor had fought in the Revolutionary War), his knowledge of blacks' participation in their own liberation in the Civil
War, and his constant reminders *why* black Americans should
fight ("if we fight we'll learn the fighting game and cease to be so
'aisly lynched,'")[2] his stand is not so unusual. Many liberals of that
day similarly shifted, the closer the war came to America.

He traveled again to Europe after the war in 1919 to investigate
racist treatment of the black troops he had urged to enter the war,
and was disgusted at what he found. The same year he helped
organize in Paris the second Pan-African Congress, and would
later aid in forming two more congresses in 1923 and 1927.
Further evidence of his widening world reputation and increasing
sympathies for socialist-communist experimentation can be seen in
his first trip to Soviet Russia in 1926. His many-pronged assault on
racism in America continued to be cultural as well as political. For
the fiftieth anniversary of the Emancipation Proclamation he
wrote in 1913 a pageant glorifying black history called "The Star
of Ethiopia." Performances of this work in New York and elsewhere over the years were always popularly received according to
Du Bois, but its production costs limited its presentation. He
helped found in Harlem in 1926 the prize-winning Krigwa
Players, but perhaps his favorite project during these years was the
unfortunately short-lived *Brownie's Book*, a charming magazine
primarily for black children. Helped by Augustus Dill as business
manager and Jessie Fauset, Du Bois's protégé, as literary editor,
Du Bois wrote a column of short, pointed comments for the
magazine in addition to selecting many of its stories, poems, and
pictures. A remark of his printed in March 1920 is typically
barbed and clear: "There were 65 persons lynched without trial in
the United States during the year 1920. No other civilized country
has such a record."

Du Bois felt that he needed to defend his people not only from
murderous attacks by whites, but from misguided attempts at
salvation proposed by various black leaders. Just as his opposition
to Booker T. Washington's accommodationist theories contained
some praise for what he considered Washington's just concern for

the working Negro, so were his attacks upon the voluntary removal to Africa schemes of Marcus Garvey qualified by his awareness that Garvey based such social and political theories as he possessed upon a high concept of racial pride. From the time Garvey contacted Du Bois in 1916 on behalf of his "Universal Negro Improvement Association" with its plan of mass migration to Africa as the ultimate solution to the problems of the race in America, Du Bois remained cautious and skeptical. He questioned the soundness of the Association's organization and its fiscal integrity. When Garvey's plan folded following various federal indictments in 1922, Du Bois was not surprised. Thereafter, while he remained sharp in his repugnance toward the "mere rhodo-montade and fatuous propaganda on which Garveyism was based," he praised Garvey's insistence that "a black skin was in itself a sort of patent to nobility," and that black folk should be proud of their African ancestors.[3]

Ironically, the issue of racial separation upon which he and Garvey seemed to disagree, caused Du Bois's first tenure with the NAACP to founder and eventually forced his separation from that organization in 1934. There had always been measures upon which the NAACP's leadership disagreed, for example, the con-flict between socialists such as Du Bois and Mary Ovington and procapitalists such as Du Bois's beloved friend Joel Spingarn over the economic-political system that would best ensure civil rights for blacks. During the Depression in the 1930s these differences were intensified because of the dwindling resources of the move-ment and because, although the organization had won numerous battles chipping away at the massive wall containing blacks in America, no great breach had yet been made in that wall: federal antilynching legislation was blocked, and still decades away were basic civil liberties that would legislate against the injustices blacks faced commonly and daily North and South, such as the obstacles to equal housing.

Beginning around 1932 following a speech Du Bois made at the NAACP's annual conference in which he called for a more vigorous and positive program of action—one which would force legal conflict rather than wait for it to arise—it became clear that major disagreements existed between factions within the NAACP that perhaps could not be resolved. These factions were not racial as much as they were ideological. Du Bois's plans for the Associa-tion as they evolved during the period and climaxing in an open dispute in 1934, called essentially for greater emphasis to be placed upon a strategy that temporarily but necessarily accepted black segregation and made of it a source of black social, economic, and political power. In the complicated and unfortunately bruising infighting that followed, Walter White and Isadore Martin, both of whom were black, vigorously opposed Du Bois, as did his old friends Mary White Ovington and Joel Spingarn. Du Bois also desired a greater role in decision-making processes within the NAACP for (mainly black) rank-and-file members. He was similarly opposed by a majority of the board in this.

As editor of *Crisis* he felt free publicly to criticize the ideas of those who opposed him, and at this point years of personal antagonism and ideological disagreement between Du Bois and various board members proved too much for the tension-wracked organization to bear. Something had to give, and that something was Du Bois. He resigned both from the editorship of *Crisis* and the board of the NAACP. His loss was lamented with sincere regrets and one suspects many an inward sigh of relief. But anyone expecting that Du Bois would now retire as a grand old but slightly tarnished warrior beyond his prime would have been greatly disappointed. Set loose from the NAACP but not out to pasture, the veteran fighter and accomplished scholar had yet another amazing three decades of productive activity to live through. He joined the NAACP when he was relatively young, and when he left it he was old, but far from finished.

I   *The Historian as Romantic Novelist*

Du Bois never permitted his demanding career with the NAACP and as a campaigner for civil rights to prevent him from continuing his efforts as a writer to express himself and to battle racism. In 1911 he published his first novel, *The Quest of the Silver Fleece*. Written with the same intensity and sense of high purpose but lacking the impact and artistry of his best nonfiction, his novels are nonetheless an important aspect of his literary career. At their best—and his first novel was clearly his most successful— they are interesting and informative attempts at fusing nineteenth-century romantic melodrama with the novel of ideas whose underlying aim is to examine the social and political forces that direct and sometimes control character. The major characters in

Du Bois's fiction seem spawned by the sentimental tradition. They lead emotional lives that are all peaks and valleys, they experience events that cause them either ecstasy or despair. They are conspired against by sinister forces of cunning and implacable evil, they swear mighty oaths and dream glorious dreams. But amid much fustian and rantipole, Du Bois provides his readers with a solid and thought-provoking background of the forces in American society that did in fact conspire against the Negro, showing behind the melodrama that dominates his fiction a picture of real and prevailing conditions affecting black life, sómething few novelists of his day were aware of or intrigued by.

The Quest of the Silver Fleece is a typical if superior Du Bois novel. It was seriously conceived and seriously worked out, but it is not a work of art. It should be viewed as a popular novel intended for a large and not necessarily sophisticated audience, dealing with an unpopular but important subject, how Negro life was controlled by Northern industrialists and Southern plantation capitalists at the turn of the century. Although he took a long time to complete the work (he refers to it in a letter written in 1905),[4] it contains the same flaws that would hamper all his fiction: characters who generally embody only the most fundamental distinctions between good and evil, and who sometimes seem to operate more for authorial convenience than by internal logic; more characters and events than he could control or that he cared to analyze with the same thoroughness and awareness of human complexity that he demonstrated in his best nonfiction; language whose formality seems too often inflated, or just plain corny. That the sources of Du Bois's novelistic craft lay in bygone days rather than in the practice of such contemporaries as James Joyce or D. H. Lawrence is made painfully evident by his continued use of capitalized abstractions such as "the End. . . . great Happiness. . . . the handwriting of Destiny. . . . Work. . . . Life. . . . the Vision. . . . Truth and Goodness and Love. . . ." Many of these abstractions are connected to each other—the Way is achieved through Sacrifice, for example—further vitiating the novel's power as a realistic work dealing in particulars.

Yet Du Bois's overwriting is often part of the special world he generates as a creative writer. The Negro characters he describes and their white tormentors and occasionally friends live in a land of terrifying extremes, a passionately heightened world, where little is normal, where (as a character suggests in one of the most

effective segments of the book, portraying a superficially simple
Negro social gathering) even ordinary conversation cannot escape
the obsession with race that so sharply stimulates and flatly
depresses the spirits of the book's characters. The world of his
racial conflict is a world of excess where melodrama is common
and sentiment is nearly always violent.

The main flow of the novel follows the growth of Bles (from
Blessed) Alwyn and his fated love, the swamp girl Zora. When the
book opens Bles is a fifteen-year-old Negro boy from Georgia who
has left home and come to Alabama to attend a school for Negroes
run by Miss Smith, an old spinster from New England whose
Puritan sense of mission and sympathy for the underprivileged
have led her to devote her life to trying to help black boys and girls
secure an education. Miss Smith is the kind of heroic white woman
Du Bois wrote about in *The Souls of Black Folk*, whom he would
write about again, for example, in *Black Reconstruction*, and for
whom he held the highest admiration. One of the novel's plots
centers around her nearly impossible attempt to keep her school
open in spite of the opposition of hostile Southerners and ignorant
Northerners.

In his goodness, his zeal for self-improvement, his almost
constant naiveté, Bles is similar to the nice young man who strives
for and deserves success in much late-nineteenth-century fiction.
It is obvious but still important to note that he was black, creating
in him a revealing and rare type to white audiences, and an
effective model for black youths who could never, as did so many
of Horatio Alger's protagonists, get ahead by marrying the boss's
daughter.

Before he arrives at Miss Smith's door, Bles meets Zora, the
novel's strongest and most interesting character. Bles first sees Zora
dancing for white men in the cabin of her "mammy," the witchlike
hag, Elspeth. Zora seems a more sexually precocious version of
W. H. Hudson's Rima the Bird Girl, a kind of nature-sprite who
had a birdlike laugh and singing voice. Bles is stunned when he
first sees Zora, "black, and lithe, and tall, and willowy. Her
garments twined and flew around the delicate moulding of her
dark, young, half-naked limbs." Zora's sensuous appeal is emphasized throughout the novel as she and Bles befriend each other, fall
in love, work together to harvest the Silver Fleece (cotton) of the
book's title, split up and travel their separate ways because Bles
discovers that Zora is sexually tainted (by the whites for whom she

in her ignorance danced), and ultimately return to each other older and far wiser. But Zora is not merely a physical woman, some kind of erotic goddess promising great fertility. She is well educated—first at Miss Smith's school, and then as a serving girl and traveling companion for the jaded, world-weary Mrs. Vanderpool. She reads Plato, Gorki, and Herbert Spencer, and demonstrates greater intelligence and leadership capacity than Bles himself. There is a definite feminist strain to the novel, part of a secondary but constant motif in Du Bois's writings, depicting the intellectual competence of women and their need for independence and equality.

Miss Smith's school is located in the heart of the black belt. The region is called Tooms County, and it is very nearly a tomb for the black people who live there in virtual slavery. As wheat is the symbolic center of Frank Norris's *The Octopus*, cotton is the crop fought over in *The Quest of the Silver Fleece*, the material prize around which social and economic forces swirl, a symbol of great wealth and of a power compelling and sometimes trapping those who work to produce or sell it. The cotton's growth is sung in lyrical outbursts, the crop's transformations from seed to baled fleece to rich textile are chronicled as the progress of a god, described as closely as the evolution of the novel's hero and heroine from raw youths to race leaders. The novel's quest is a quest for Zora and Bles to develop and mature and finally to find each other, but also a quest for the force they represent—the Negro—to control what is necessary to determine the conditions of its existence. Cotton is the key to these quests, the central image binding all the sprawling action of the book and the disparate lives of its characters together.[5] Its growth is determined by climatic conditions difficult to harness and usually impossible to dominate, yet the prize of wealth it can bring is capable of control, and the ways Northern industrialists and financial interests conspire with Southern plantation capitalists and the emerging poor white class to maintain white supremacy and thus secure the crop's profit is investigated with far more penetration than is the rather sentimental relationship between the book's hero and heroine. The cotton brings together Bles and Zora who work with each other to master its growth, but the alliance instituted by Zora between the poor whites and blacks, who recognize their common upper-class oppressors in the struggle to control the crop's wealth, is fleeting. This union which Du Bois so often dreamed about is quickly exploded by capitalist exploitation of the poor whites' irrational hatred of blacks.

The plot upon which these political and economic conflicts is hung is filled with incident as first Bles and then Zora leaves Alabama for Washington and the great world. Minor characters exemplify subsidiary viewpoints and social stereotypes to flesh out the great thematic battles in the novel, the quest for cotton's power, the determined drive toward black self-realization. A number of minor black characters show how the pressures of being black in America at the turn of the century could modify or warp character—the very intelligent and opportunistic Caroline Wynn, blocked from the role in life her brains should have guaranteed her because she is both black and a woman; cynical and cunning Sam Stillings, who is willing to endure practically any humiliation to work at the fringes of white power and thus pick up crumbs to enrich himself (the phrase "up from servility" that is used to describe his social ascent seems a parody of Washington's *Up From Slavery*); the unctuous and traitorous Preacher Jones, the kind of black Judas that Frank Yerby would later write so much about in his popular novels.[6]

Secondary white characters similarly represent classes of whites who are part of the web of bigotry strung through American society: the conniving banker Mr. Easterly (whose name suggests his region); the played-out socialite Mrs. Vanderpool; Miss Smith's corrupt brother Senator Smith; the poor white Tolliver who "hated 'niggers' only a shade more than he hated white aristocrats."

Du Bois referred in *Dusk of Dawn* to *The Quest of the Silver Fleece* as "really an economic study of some merit," and perhaps the most impressive element of the novel is the way he shows how cotton dominated much Southern life of the period, how the lives of blacks and whites intertwined in furthering the processes of its cultivation and selling. Broderick praises the variety of themes the book encompasses including "the thirst for knowledge among young Negroes; the persistent slave mentality among the older ones," and the ways blacks and whites mutually deceived each other within the uneasy hegemony the whites controlled in the South. In some way or other, however, all these themes, including the struggle for self-realization engaged in so painfully by Zora and Bles, are related to the conflict between blacks and whites over economic self-determination, which in turn centers upon control of the cotton crop. As one character baldly phrases it, "cheap cotton is built upon cheap niggers." To keep "niggers" cheap, Du Bois shows that the South, aided by Northern bankers, industrialists, and politicians, will defraud, disfranchise, and terrorize them, and either prevent or pervert their education. The novel taught that the way for Southern blacks to break the bondage they were forced to endure lay in personal sacrifice and striving for education and greatly strengthened solidarity to achieve the political and communal strength necessary to implement any social change. An alliance some day with poor whites similarly oppressed by the Northern and Southern capitalistic combine is suggested more as a hope than as an immediate goal of the black community. Individual whites such as Miss Smith might help, but the thrust for liberation had to be generated within the black civilization, led by specially gifted and educated individuals such as Zora and Bles.

Du Bois's fiction is not comparable to that of his American contemporaries such as Henry James, Theodore Dreiser, Edith Wharton, or Frank Norris, all of whom possessed greater technical skill, ability to characterize vividly, firmer control over the action presented in their novels. And certainly Charles Chesnutt and Paul Dunbar surpassed him in depicting individual black lives with subtlety and the feel of reality. But in the kind of novel Du Bois wrote in *Quest of the Silver Fleece*—a black problem novel in the style of a romance—he is a noteworthy practitioner. He avoided for the most part describing the "life among the lowly" that his earlier books proved he knew so well and that the naturalistic writers of his day and later black writers such as Claude McKay and Richard Wright would powerfully exploit; instead he employed idealized black characters who could serve as models for his black readers, in a plot whose outlines are epic-romantic but whose foundation is based upon the economic and political realities he devoted his life to exposing. Du Bois may have described the romance between Bles and Zora in glossy, conventional, love-story fashion, but the grit of their black lives was not ordinary to slick fiction. The humiliation of riding in a Jim Crow car, and the sight of lynched black bodies hanging from an Alabama pine, were not part of the world of most lovers in popular escapist fiction.

There is a power contained in *The Quest of the Silver Fleece* that Du Bois never again achieved in his other four novels. He

penetrates beyond the veil of race mentioned so often in the novel
separating black life from white, and presents a number of
characters (mainly women) who take on lives of their own. He
also removed other veils from American life—political, economic,
moral—to show the corruption that is necessary and profitable to
keep Negroes in an inferior position in American society. Some
larger symbols in the book also achieve definite power: the cotton
fleece that lures so many men and women to reward or doom; the
primal swamp closely associated with Zora and Bles, where they
grow their special almost magical cotton crop and where eventually a small black community stakes its hopes for survival and
prosperity—a fertile, dangerous, tricky place that can harbor and
sustain black life if properly mastered, but only if properly
mastered, like America itself. In many ways these positive elements compensate for the novel's often wooden dialogue, frequently one-dimensional characterizations, and the too-obvious
manipulation of plot action. Viewed as a fictional counterpart to
his three best earlier works, the book is a clumsy, overwritten
failure. Seen as a novel that could have provided a larger popular
white audience and a smaller black audience with an enjoyable if
romantic story exposing the political realities undergirding race
relations in the South and North, the novel gains in stature.

II *The African Heritage:* The Negro

Du Bois wrote about black life from many perspectives. Perhaps
he should not have taken upon himself single-handedly the
monumental task of rehabilitating the Negro past and present, but
he felt, beyond a strong personal compulsion to do so, a moral
obligation to present to the world a full and positive image of
black life. *The Negro* (1915) constituted another aspect of that
image.

Called by historian Herbert Aptheker the "first overall examination of the history of African and African-derived peoples,"[7] the
book was an attempt in brief space and for a popular audience to
present the general outlines of Negro and more particularly
African history at a time when information on the subject was
woefully scanty and often distorted. Du Bois had to counter in the
book the kind of generally held assumption as that contained in
Senator James Vardamen's remark in Congress a year before
publication of *The Negro* that the race "never had any civilization

except that which has been inculcated by a superior race," that the Negro's civilizations lasted "only so long as he is in the hands of the white man who inculcates it. When left to himself he has universally gone back to the barbarism of the jungle."

To combat such vicious and destructive assertions, Du Bois briefly narrated the past of African kingdoms such as ancient Ghana, Mali, and Songhay; discussed the role that Africa played in Western, Egyptian, and Muslim history; described the sophisticated polity of the African states and the high culture of their peoples; and characterized the various physical types that have inhabited Sub-Saharan Africa, exploding the myth of a single or standard Negro type and devastating the concept of racial superiority based upon physique. He insisted upon recognizing African artistic achievements, for example, in mask making and metal work. He distinguished between the slave trade as it existed in Africa and many Western states prior to European intervention in Africa, and the variety of slavery that evolved around the 1600s, the period of the great expansion of Western Europe and the Americas. This expansion Du Bois noted was made possible by the black trade which brought wealth in materials and especially labor to the white kingdoms. The institution of slavery created by the West and peopled by Africans was vastly more damaging to the Negro psyche and to the African homeland than the earlier, more limited and less racist strain, according to Du Bois. The slave trade he calls Africa's "heart disease," and to that disease he attributes the "uprooting of ancient African culture, leaving only misty reminders of the ruin in the customs and work of the people."

After discussing the great African past and wretched colonial present, Du Bois briefly sketched the history of the Negro in the New World, focusing especially upon slave rebellions in the West Indies and upon the heroic Negro attempts to rehabilitate themselves during the years following the Civil War when they were permitted some limited self-determination, a tragic period he had written of before in *The Souls of Black Folk* and would return to several times later in his career, most notably in *Black Reconstruction*.

The book's greatest virtue resides in its positive picture of black history. Clear and compact, it is an amazing work for a nonscholar in African history—especially one with little time in his life for deep or original research. It successfully sketches the broad outlines of African history, stressing the substantiality of African political and economic achievement, and to a lesser degree African artistic attainments, generally denigrated or unknown in the West (except in a few centers that displayed pieces stolen from their African country of origin). The work is also commendable for raising issues still debated by scholars with a greater background of information than Du Bois had access to. Whether or not the African social fabric was rent as violently as Du Bois claims from the depradations of the slavers, the fact that he examined the effects of the forced diaspora upon African society provided stimulating thought for future scholars. His investigation of African survivals in the New World—in religion, for example—foreshadowed the work of later researchers such as Melville Herskovits in *Dahomey, An Ancient West African Kingdom* (1938), or *The Myth of the Negro Past* (1958). Occasionally the sly humor he slipped into his text ridiculing Western bigotry is therapeutic, for example, when he mentions how "the Christian church gravely defended Negro slavery and oppression as the rightful curse of God upon the descendents of a son [Ham] who had been disrespectful to his drunken father!"

But in other ways it was unfortunate that Du Bois felt he had to write the book. He was not a scholar in the field, and he was again at the mercy of his sources, which are sparse, randomly employed, and error-ridden.[8]

In his valuable introduction to a recent (1970) edition of the text, George Shepperson points out certain strange constructions Du Bois employed, such as "La Bantu" and "Zulu-Kaffir." What Du Bois meant by his references to ancient African "industrial cities" and "industrial development," to the "industrial democracy" or "city democracy" of the Yoruba is uncertain and greatly needs clarification. More perplexing are Du Bois's claims that most of tropical Africa has a "warm, dry climate" and that a physical fact underlying "all African history" is "the absence of interior barriers," when much of the land is very hot and very rainy and filled with physical obstacles.

Sometimes Du Bois accepts questionable conjectures about black history that have little factual support, for example, the opinion of E. W. Blyden that the features of the Sphinx at Giza "are decidedly of the African or Negro Type" (though Du Bois also argued that there was no true Negro type). These conjectures, however, are certainly no less valid than many white assumptions that minimized African intelligence or culture. Occasionally his limitations as a scholar combine with his tendency to pursue private theories of African history, to produce simply inaccurate conclusions. Because he believed slavery devastated Africa and caused degeneration in its social systems, he saw "the Yoruban culture, with its city democracy, its elevated religious ideas, its finely organized industry, and its noble art" replaced by the hegemony of the Ashanti and Dahomey with their "orgies of war and blood sacrifice." The evolution he describes does terrible disservice to the realities of both Ashanti and Dahomey history, distorting each beyond recognition, and even ignoring the liberationist struggle of the Ashanti in 1900.

The Negro was not definitive, as were *The Suppression of the African Slave-Trade* and *The Philadelphia Negro*. As a popular history it was highly informative, and contained none of the inaccurate and repugnant white supremicist assertions that marred several generations of texts on the subject. To whites it offered a corrective view of black history, and for the black reader it was an exciting adventure, an intellectual counterpart to the discovery of fabulous and uncharted lands. The black scholar and Africanist William Leo Hansberry is only one black historian who has left a touching tribute to Du Bois's inspirational accomplishment in the book, telling how as a young boy his mind was fired by Du Bois's narrative of the great black past, and relating how Du Bois stimulated him to proceed farther where the magnificent teacher had first explored even though as is true of many explorers Du Bois did not describe the terrain he found with absolute fidelity.

Intensely involved with destroying the warped image of the Negro that had been fixed in the popular lore of the West, Du Bois defended blackness in the Negro by pointing to its positive accomplishments and not by slashing at Western achievement. Although the last pages of his rapid tour of black history include the assertion that "the future world will, in all reasonable probability, be what colored men make it," since throughout the world the so-called colored races are most populous, he also issued in his book a call for racial harmony. "The Pan-African movement," he stated, will not "be merely a narrow racial propaganda." All people are linked, he says in the "unity of the working classes everywhere, a unity of the colored races, a new unity of men."

III   *Darker Souls:* Darkwater

Darkwater (1920) is the second of Du Bois's racial biographies. Like *The Souls of Black Folk* it contains a selection of previously published work newly edited and organized for book publication and augmented by fresh material. Once again Du Bois presented his growing audience with carefully selected vignettes from his personal life together with interludes where he becomes a representative Negro recounting experiences common to the race; he combines these narratives with short stories, poems, and more formal sociocultural essays on aspects of the black existence, to produce a mixed literary form attaining unity through Du Bois's overall focus on the nature of black life, and through the controlled and rather somber tone with which he generally treats his material.

The book differs from its predecessor in its increased radicalism, its almost unrelieved pessimism, and its nearly constant bitterness. Although in *Darkwater* Du Bois writes specifically of needed economic and political reforms and though clearly he was by no means ready to surrender to the white capitalistic society that subjugated black Americans in its midst, he is far more insistent upon portraying the horrors of Negro life than he had been in *The Souls of Black Folk,* and more precise in calling for a different kind of government—a socialistic one—to redress the problems of black men and women. *Darkwater* is also more uneven in its literary accomplishments than the earlier work.

The bitterness pervading the book is not surprising. Though Du Bois was an important public figure in 1920 in a way he had not been in 1903, although his life was filled with all the recognition a black man could hope for in America, in his fiftieth year the race was perhaps worse off that it had been when *The Souls of Black Folk* was written. Twenty years of hope and work and sacrifice and ill-treatment had advanced it no farther than it had been at the start of the century. Always in the South and sometimes in the North too, blacks were disfranchised and packed into ghettoes and Jim Crowed. In 1917 in East St. Louis, white strikers started a riot that ended in a pogrom leaving 125 Negroes killed. In 1919 the Ku Klux Klan was stronger than it had been since Reconstruction days, seventy Negroes were lynched nation-wide, and the country shuddered through at least twenty-five race riots. Claude McKay's memorable sonnet "If We Must Die" struck a note of desperate defiance that year while the NAACP chipped away at the great wall of injustice and indifference surrounding Negroes. Du Bois's anger was more than ever justified during this time of blood.

He frames his anger in *Darkwater* by employing at the start of his book a statement of faith in God and in the brotherhood of man, called "Credo," and by placing at the book's conclusion "A Hymn to the Peoples" which admits the weakness of all peoples and beseeches the "Human God . . . to make Humanity divine." "Credo" especially has been much admired by speakers who seek to add oratorical reverberations to their public utterances. Typical of Du Bois, it combines the spirit of what might loosely be called today negritude ("Especially do I believe in the Negro Race: in the beauty of its genius, the sweetness of its soul") with an old fashioned Calvinistic drive ("I believe in service . . . for Work is Heaven, Idleness Hell, and Wage is the 'Well done!' of the Master").

But the spirit of brotherhood does not pervade the essays enclosed by these two pieces. As if to spotlight how terrible present-day life had become, the first of the essays, "The Shadow of Years," offers a softened version of Du Bois's life until the Niagara Movement (1905–1909/10) and his severance from Atlanta University in 1910. As Broderick has pointed out, Du Bois tended to minimize the hardships and difficulties of his earliest years, viewing them as a time of almost unbroken triumph punctuated by a few unpleasant incidents of racial prejudice. "I willed and lo!" he writes, "I was walking beneath the elms of Harvard,—the name of allurement, the college of my youngest, wildest visions! I needed money; scholarships and prizes fell into my lap. . . . I asked for a fellowship and got it." His life had not been that easy, but the essay makes it seem as though it had been.

His childhood years are similarly described through a more romantic haze than in *The Souls of Black Folk*. "I was born by a golden river and in the shadow of two great hills. . . . The house was quaint, with clapboards running up and down, neatly trimmed, and there were five rooms, a tiny porch, a rosy front yard, and unbelievably delicious strawberries in the rear." Perhaps the land of his childhood was as bucolic as this, but one wonders how open about his youth he is being when he writes about his mother and his triumphant graduation from high school that "it was her great day and that very year she lay down with a sigh of content and has not yet awakened. I felt a certain gladness to see

her, at last, at peace. . . . Of my own loss I had then little
realization." The description of his father Alfred also fits pleas-
antly into the rosy vision of his early years he creates in the essay,
"small and beautiful of face and feature, just tinted with the sun
. . . a dreamer,—romantic, indolent, kind, unreliable." One
suspects this vision of his life with its memories of his mother's
death so painless to him, and of his beautiful but totally vanished
father, emerged from the dreams of an older man who did not
want to reveal all the secret turmoils of his starting out, even to
himself. Or perhaps Du Bois is setting up the reader for the racial
horrors he will suddenly plunge into. There is certainly some
unconscious irony in Du Bois's lovely description of his childhood,
for later we learn that the "golden river" of his "birth was golden
because of the woolen and paper waste that soiled it." And we
learn too that many of the ancestors that he lovingly describes in
the chapter died worn down from poverty or the abrasion of living
in a white world, or like his father drifted away into the haze of
the unknown.

"A Litany at Atlanta," the prose poem immediately following
Du Bois's reminiscences, dispells any nostalgic aura "The Shadow
of Years" might have created. Supposedly written on a train
returning Du Bois to riot-torn Atlanta in 1906, the poem constitutes a shocking and valid indictment of the South and of white
Atlanta specifically, for permitting what Du Bois later termed, in
his novel *The Ordeal of Mansart,* four days of "drunken, sadistic
orgy of murder, theft and maiming" engaged in by a lawless
rabble but caused really by decades of political demagoguery,
racist journalism, and respectable white compliance to the systematic degrading of the Negro. "A Litany at Atlanta" follows the
standard leader-audience response of its liturgical model and
makes the religious traditions of the form part of the poem's attack
upon whoever is responsible for the slaughter of black sinners
whose guilt seems slight compared to the "devils . . . who nursed
them in crime and fed them on injustice. . . . Who ravished and
debauched their mothers and their grandmothers." Du Bois peti-
tions God to punish black sinners but questions whether the truly
guilty are not escaping free, "the innocent . . . crucified for the
guilt of the untouched guilty." A black man lies maimed and
broken and murdered, he says, "his wife naked to shame, his
children to poverty and evil," and yet there is no divine vengeance.
"Doth not this justice of hell stink in Thy nostrils, O God?"

Thus the petition becomes almost a parody of prayer in prayer form, a Job's cry for justice to a "Silent God," perhaps even to a "God of the fathers" who is "dead." The poem's language is greatly heightened, but the powerfully wrought intensity is here justified by the enormity of the crime which is its subject. When Du Bois declares "Bewildered we are and passion-tossed, mad with the madness of a mobbed and mocked and murdered people," his portentous wording is at a level with the calamity he describes. His fury is contained and advanced by the traditional biblical form he employs, which helps prevent his anger from becoming rant. Further, there is irony in his version of the form when he adapts it to his polemical use. One section, for example, contains the chanted leader's speech and audience response:

> From lust of power and lust of blood,—
> *Great God, deliver us!*
> From lust of power and lust of gold,—
> *Great God, deliver us!*
> From the leagued lying of despot and of brute,—
> *Great God, deliver us!*

The petition is actually a condemnation, a damning of the white society that had brought about the rioting, not a plea for mercy. Du Bois wrote other poems during his career, but none as effective as "A Litany at Atlanta."[9]

Du Bois journeyed to the other side of the racial "veil" (a word used throughout *Darkwater* as it had been in many of his earlier works) in the chapter that follows, "The Souls of White Folk." Here he surveys the white Western mentality, its colonialism, its hypocrisy, and ultimately its madness. The essay is not as historically detailed as similar segments in *The Souls of Black Folk* typically were, but its indictment of white society is more clear. Particular objects of Du Bois's hatred are white arrogance and the "cruelty, barbarism, and murder done to men and women of Negro descent" by the supposedly superior white society. He ridicules America's crusade to "make the 'World Safe for Democracy'" and looks on mildly amazed during World War I when whites stopped murdering blacks for a time, to kill each other. Sarcastically he writes about how the white "supermen and world-mastering demi-gods" would not listen to "low tongues of ours . . . we . . . folk of simpler soul and more primitive type," and admits to the "contempt" black people felt witnessing the "misera-

ble failure" of "white Christianity." Western society he says is built
upon the exploitation of men and women of color, black, brown,
yellow, and red. World War I, he claims (in an argument he
would often repeat), was caused by the squabble among white
nations for control of the colored labor market.

Thus the white world is observed as a sham, its civilized nations
"crazed beasts." Obviously Du Bois's voice had become more
assertive than its relatively muted tone in *The Souls of Black Folk*; it
was striking again the bolder notes of *John Brown*. "No nation," he
concludes, is less qualified for the role of peacemaker that America
aspired to after World War I. "For more than two or more centuries
America has marched proudly in the van of human hatred,—
making bonfires of human flesh and laughing at them hideously."
Du Bois's strong language here and the feelings it reveals demonstrate that the scholar who wrote the relatively moderate *Philadelphia Negro* had evolved into a more outspoken and bitterly defiant
spokesman, a Negro for the new age of the 1920s.

The succeeding essays, poems, and stories in *Darkwater* expand
upon and sometimes qualify but never really change the picture of
black life Du Bois presents in "A Litany at Atlanta" and "The
Souls of White Folk." The poem "The Riddle of the Sphinx" tells of
the "white world's vermin and filth," and the essay "The Hands of
Ethiopia" calls for "a new African World State" that will enable
Africans to determine their own objectives and the nature of their
political existence. "Of Work and Wealth" opens with as fine a
brief description of how it feels to be a teacher as has been written
(the teacher "tends to be stilted, almost dishonest, veiling himself
before those awful eyes") and then discusses the terrible necessity
Du Bois felt as a black teacher to lie in response to the basic
question his black students asked: "Do you trust white people?"
(You answer yes, he says, though the students know you lie. You
answer yes for the students' "salvation and the world's.") Then,
under the guise of explaining what the black teacher must teach to
his students, Du Bois discusses black-white labor relations in East
St. Louis that led to racial war in the city. "The Servant in the
House" similarly begins on a personal note, relating the painful
comedy Du Bois experienced after a speech on disfranchisement
when a white woman came up to him and asked, "do you know
where I can get a good colored cook?"

"Of the Ruling of Men" discusses the black need for voting
rights, and again demonstrates Du Bois's advancing liberalism as

he grew older. In *The Philadelphia Negro* and elsewhere in his early works he agreed that probably "unqualified" Negro voters should not have been allowed to vote had white citizens unprepared for intelligent participation in politics been disqualified also. Now he disavows any infringement upon voting rights based on property or education. His reasoning is that though "we say easily . . . 'the ignorant ought not to vote,' we should say 'no civilized state should have citizens too ignorant to participate in government.' " The ballot, he suggests, is the greatest hope the poor and undereducated possess to attain their material and intellectual needs.

"The Immortal Child" very clearly parallels the essay "Of Alexander Crummel" in *The Souls of Black Folk*. It tells of the few triumphs of the black English composer Coleridge-Taylor—practically unknown today, narrating the outlines of his life in a manner similar to that of a funeral elegy, somberly hinting of his existence "within the veil," declaring that he was lucky not to be born in the United States where his career would have been even more blighted from the start, and sadly lamenting the death which cut him off from the full achievement later years, Du Bois claims, would have brought him. The essay is less powerful than its earlier counterpart, perhaps because its tone is so solemn and partly because its unity is disturbed when Du Bois concludes it with an extended discussion of how black children should be educated at home and in school. The book's last essay, "Of Beauty and Death," is similarly split in its focus, interspersing real and very chilling incidents of bigotry Negroes might meet as an ordinary part of their day with short historical narratives about the racism black soldiers met in World War I, and pretentiously wordy flights about Beauty and Death.

Although *Darkwater* is an uneven book, it contains much good writing about a variety of subjects. Two concerns, the status of women and socialism, while not new to Du Bois, are more pervasive than in his earlier major works, and through the assertiveness and hope with which they are presented, help balance the often negative and death-obsessed tone of the text.

A number of essays and one entire chapter, "The Damnation of Women," deal with women's rights. Agitation leading to the granting of the vote to women in 1920 made the topic a popular one, but Du Bois had for a long time been interested in the issue, perhaps ever since observing the plight of his own mother whose rights and alternatives were so arbitrarily limited by society. His interest extended to all women held subservient by their designated role in society. In "The Damnation of Women" he compares women's need for the ballot to the need of black Americans. Just as women were told that everything they could do for themselves with the ballot could be done for them by men, so were Negroes. Similarly, franchised men cried that "women do not want the ballot" just as whites claimed that "the 'best' Negroes stay out of politics." Du Bois is uncompromising and prescient in his demands for women, admitting that enfranchisement of women will cost something and "may even change the present status of family life . . . interfere with the present prerogatives of men and probably for some time to come annoy them considerably." But the change, he firmly states, is absolutely necessary and just. "We cannot imprison women again in a home or require them all on pain of death to be nurses and housekeepers." Du Bois, as did Frederick Douglass before him, championed women's rights along with Negro rights.

Darkwater also reveals Du Bois's evolving sympathy with socialism if not yet with Marxism itself, though in "Of the Ruling of Men" he demonstrates sympathy with the Marxist goal of securing "the greatest good of all . . . [by] doing away with private property in machines and materials." His critique of American and European capitalism is clearly from left of center. Industry, he argues, runs the country and is "in the hands of the few," producing an ill-concealed monarchy or aristocracy which must be replaced by a true democracy that will determine such matters as the distribution of goods. Du Bois proposes ultimately a mixture of reforms not completely socialistic but tending toward socialism, including the "increase of public democratic ownership of industry, beginning with the simplest utilities and monopolies . . . taxation to limit inheritance . . . a 'single tax' on monopolized land values," and "the training of the public in business technique by co-operation in buying and selling." His last measure shows that the new state he imagined would leave room for private enterprise. He was aware that "some Socialists openly excluded Negroes and Asiatics from their scheme" of civic betterment, but asserted that "perhaps the finest contribution of current Socialism to the world is neither its light nor its dogma, but the idea back of its one mighty word—Comrade!" Thus his dream of a new society embraces racial compatability.

Had Du Bois not included in *Darkwater* some rather pretentiously obscure poetry and some painfully clear allegorical fiction, the book would have more successfully achieved its object. Yet, perhaps this kind of book would not have accurately represented him, for he was a man of many and unequal talents, whose dreamy aestheticism possibly humanizes even as it verbally clutters his rigorous and cutting social criticism. Even amid the failures of his short fiction in *Darkwater* at least one interesting work appears, "The Comet," investigating the fate of a black man and white woman who seem to be the only humans left in a world devastated by gasses from a comet's tail.[10] The two remaining people draw together as sympathetic and loving human beings until they discover that the black and white civilization outside New York still exists. In the story's conclusion the black man is nearly lynched by a white mob.

The story's language and dialogue are unequal to Du Bois's interesting theme, though perhaps never as bad as the phrasing in some of the essays, one of which describes "the sun kissing the timid dew in Central Park." A parable of the brief but perhaps inevitably doomed union of the races, the pessimistic short story lacks the power and craft found frequently throughout *Darkwater*. The book does not belong with Du Bois's best, but it is doubtful that many other writers of the day would have possessed the combined critical intelligence, the social insight, and the artistic ability to duplicate it: the book would have secured a minor reputation for many a lesser writer.

IV A Critic Divided

Perhaps the single most important body of popular writing Du Bois produced during the 1920s was his superb journalism for *Crisis*. He wrote the equivalent of volumes on topics of current and lasting interest to black Americans, especially items relating to the civil rights struggle. Dealing with a great variety of problems on almost a day-to-day basis, and demonstrating mastery of the ability to communicate with a cross section of readers, Du Bois filled *Crisis* with clear and pointed prose. Often in his articles he used materials gleaned from his academic studies, and frequently the short pieces he wrote provided him with matter he would treat later in his magazine articles and ultimately in his books (especially the "Mansart" series).

Du Bois appears to have experienced few difficulties switching from being a writer of fairly substantial literature to functioning as an editor and reporter. He used his position as editor of *Crisis* to further the development of a significant Afro-American literature, and also exercised his judgment as a literary critic in *Crisis* and in other periodicals in an attempt to direct the course of that literature. He was not as successful in this last endeavor as he was in either shifting from scholar to journalist or in using his editorial position to provide a haven for black literature. Arnold Rampersad concludes that almost from the time of its inception until Charles Johnson's *Opportunity: A Journal of Negro Life* in 1923, *Crisis* was "the most significant outlet for poems and stories written by black Americans," and in the years prior to the Harlem Renaissance was "preeminent among black publications in its encouragement of art."[11] Shaping the literary contents of *Crisis* partly by himself and partly through the aides he selected such as the anthologist and poet William Stanley Braithwaite and the novelist Jessie Fauset, Du Bois encouraged black writers such as Claude McKay, Langston Hughes, and Jean Toomer to appear before a national audience.

Critically and personally Du Bois had strong feelings toward the writers whose careers he oversaw, but to a surprising degree he did not let these feelings dictate editorial choices: he often permitted publication of writers whose objectives or techniques he did not favor. For example, although he disapproved of Jean Toomer's mystic and esoteric symbolism he still asked him in a letter of 1924 for stories. And although Du Bois's relations with Claude McKay were understandably stormy for many years—on 18 June 1928, McKay sent Du Bois an angry letter attacking Du Bois's criticism in the June 1928 *Crisis* of McKay's novel *Home to Harlem*, which stated that the book "for the most part nauseates me, and after the dirtier parts of its filth I feel like taking a bath"—as Rampersad points out, Du Bois suggested in 1933 that McKay "write a book column for the *Crisis*."[12] Similarly, although Du Bois's personal relationship with Walter White was often acidic, Du Bois could write to a student that White's novel *Fire in the Flint* was significant as a "correct portraiture" of Negro life by a black writer. Certainly Du Bois provided an arena for a number of important black writers who otherwise would have had little chance for national exposure in the white-dominated publishing and reviewing industries. Further, through the contests sponsored by *Crisis* he inspired the work of literally thousands of lesser and never-known writers who would otherwise have received little stimulus to express themselves creatively.

Du Bois's achievement as a force in black literature might have been higher had he been less confusing as a theorist. The headnote quotations to Rampersad's excellent discussion of Du Bois's criticism accurately reflect Du Bois's problem. Du Bois at once declares that the notion that "our Art and Propaganda . . . are one" is "wrong and in the end it is harmful," and then elsewhere states that "All art is propaganda." These passages about the autonomy and at the same time the responsibilities of the writer do not represent stages in Du Bois's development as a critic, but rather concurrent tendencies that existed throughout his career. While the dual emphases he placed upon the demands of both art and propaganda in the life of the artist may have helped produce in himself a writer-ideologue unusually committed to both art and politics, his divided focus as a critic could only baffle many young black writers seeking clear goals. While his advocacy of both segregation and integration can be explained, I feel, by understanding that he felt the ultimate achievement of the latter would best be expedited by the partial but immediate acceptance of the former, his divided allegiance to aesthetics and ideology is not easy—and is perhaps impossible—to resolve.

If a bridge to what seems the split in his critical thinking can be constructed, it might employ his unstated but clear awareness that as a critic (and as a writer and an activist) he was conscious of at least two audiences for literature about blacks, one within the Negro community and one outside.

In the May 1925 *Crisis* he wrote that "We are seriously crippling Negro art and literature by refusing to contemplate any but handsome heroes, unblemished heroines and flawless defenders." In a letter of 1 August 1923 to Mrs. E. A. Duffield in which he defends Langston Hughes's poetry from charges of vulgarity, Du Bois wrote that "I am absolutely convinced that the last way to conquer evil is to hide the evil from youth. The poet depicts life as it is. . . . Mr. Hughes in his strikingly beautiful poems . . . talks about prostitutes frankly" but does not make "the cabarets of Harlem beautiful and desirable." Yet in response to a 29 October 1925 letter from the novelist and critic Carl Van Vechten charging *Crisis* with harshness toward works presenting "unpleasant truths" about Negro life, Du Bois answered that work showing "the Negro to . . . disadvantage . . . has been overdone and there is almost no corresponding work on the other side." In the review of *Home to Harlem* already noted, one of Du Bois's chief criticisms is that in depicting the seamy side of Harlem McKay's book is "untrue, not so much as on account of its facts, but on account of its emphasis on glaring colors."

In other words, the Negro writer had to write what was true, for truth was of prime importance to the black audience and to the black artist. But the truth about Negro life should be ultimately positive because black Americans needed to look up in their lives and not wallow in the ugly or second-rate existence most American literature consigned Negroes to, when not portraying comical or servile blacks. It was necessary that Hughes as an artist wrote about prostitutes because they were a part of black life. Further, it was good that he did not make their world attractive, because Negroes needed to see the shabbiness of prostitution. But white society, Du Bois also suggests, is only too eager to view black sexuality with prurient interest, and is strongly conditioned to view black life as sexually loose, and so caution had to be exercised not to reinforce racist views. The black writer should aim at creating Art, one of whose components was Truth (Du Bois usually saw these terms as idealized abstractions to be capitalized), but the Truth had to be carefully modeled to further a positive view of black life and attack racism.

Du Bois also undoubtedly took into consideration the needs of the black community to be told the truth and at the same time to be protected from white stereotypes of black inferiority when he pronounced the Harlem Renaissance both a success and a failure. To the white world at large and H. L. Mencken (who had adversely criticized Negro literature) he announced that "We Negroes are quite well satisfied with our Renaissance," while for the black record he insisted that the Renaissance had failed because it was too exotic and had never been rooted deeply in black foundations."[13]

Even considering the special needs of black writers and black audiences—needs thrust upon them by the mistreatment they had experienced in American life and literature—the diverging elements of Du Bois's critical theories still seem hard to harness if treated in tandem, and excessively constraining if treated singly. His ideal, stated in the March 1915 *Crisis*, that poetry "must above all be beautiful, alluring, delicate, fine," does not harmoniously

blend with the basic premise of his 1926 speech on "The Criteria
of Negro Art" which is that "Negro art should play a central part
in the struggle for political liberation."[14]

As a practicing critic Du Bois was shrewd, spirited, cutting—
nearly always interesting and often penetrating even if wrong. His
review of Richard Wright's autobiographical *Black Boy* in the 2
March 1945 *New York Herald Tribune* is fairly representative of
his journalistic criticism. Wright was probably the best known
black writer in America at the time of the review, having
published a number of superb short stories and the very powerful
novel *Native Son* (1940). Wright had also been a member of the
Communist party, and though he had broken with the party by
this time he still considered himself something of a Marxist.

Du Bois's review, titled "Richard Wright Looks Back," makes no
use of the analytic techniques so intensively employed by various
schools of modern criticism such as the myth critics or the textual
(the so-called new) critics. Nor does his review follow the Marxist
lines established mainly during the 1920s and 1930s by such
American critics as Mike Gold or Granville Hicks. Du Bois's
approach seems closest to an older school of literary critics in
America, the New Humanists, in its strongly moralistic tone, its
double focus upon both the ethics and aesthetics of the work
examined, and its easily apparent distaste for the book's emphasis
upon sordid detail. What bothered Du Bois most about Wright's
book (generally conceded today to be one of Wright's best) was its
insistently and consistently negative image of black life coupled
with what appeared to be Wright's lack of sympathy with any
aspect of that life. Du Bois laments that Wright narrates the tale of
his grandfather, a disappointed Civil War veteran, "without
sympathy." In fact, Du Bois objects, "the Negroes whom he paints
have almost no redeeming qualities." A few work hard or have
cunning, but "none . . . is ambitious, successful, or really
intelligent." Actually, the central figure in *Black Boy*, Wright
himself, was all three, but Du Bois does not note this.

Du Bois attacks Wright primarily for projecting black life
without the faintest glimmer of pleasantness or goodness, but he
also scores Wright's view of white life which is similarly devastating. "There is not a single broad-minded, open-hearted white
person in his book," Du Bois objects. He praises Wright's "vigorous
and straightforward English," the "real beauty in his words even
when they are mingled with sadism," but clearly regrets Wright's

obsession with the "concentrated meanness, filth and despair" which to Du Bois grossly distorted reality.

Du Bois recognized, as many contemporary critics did not, that Wright's so-called "Record of Childhood and Youth" was a heavily fictionalized reminiscence: "mainly," Du Bois said, the book should be treated as "fiction or fictionalized biography." He seemed further aware how solipsistic Wright's view of Negro life actually was, how "self-centered to the exclusion of everybody and everything else" is the central character whose natural introversion is "forced back upon itself" until he becomes all that he sees around him: "The world is himself and his suffering," Du Bois observes. Had Du Bois viewed Wright's book more as a literary text shaped for certain specific artistic purposes, and less as a one-sided, unhealthy presentation of black life and white, had he pursued his insight that the work is a highly subjective fictionalization of Wright's life, he might have anticipated more recent criticism which examines Wright as an existentialist and symbolist as well as a realist. One wonders if in reviewing Wright's depressing pseudo-autobiography, Du Bois was not thinking of his own personal writings. He too had known despair and had suffered from the hatred of a violent, white world, but he had not—he felt—succumbed to the hostility around him, nor would he allow himself in depicting that world and the black world within it, to permit his audience to think that all he saw was meanness and decay, and all he felt was a loss of sympathy.

V   *The Educator Writes:* The Gift of Black Folk

Confused or perceptive as a critic, Du Bois was still operating in a role familiar to him, that of teacher. And the purpose of his criticism was identical to that of his journalism and of the books he wrote, to educate black and white America in the varieties of black experience. The rhetorical strategies he employed in his different works he might alter to suit his audiences, but his aim was always the same, to make America and the world aware of the conditions of black life past and present, and to suggest to white and black Americans what that condition might be in the future. Some of his books, such as *Darkwater*, were personal, discursive, and highly polemical. Others, such as *The Negro* or *The Gift of Black Folk* (1924), were more like introductory school textbooks in nature. As Truman Nelson writes in his introduction to *The Gift of Black Folk*, "almost every one of these works came into existence to fill a need and meet some daily imperative to nourish and advance the will of the black people to achieve full equality in a society which had denied it to them since 1619."

Relying heavily upon the Atlanta University publications, his own earlier research, and the investigations of black historians such as Carter Woodson, Alice Dunbar Nelson, Benjamin Brawley, and George Washington Williams, Du Bois compiled in *The Gift of Black Folk* introductory historical essays on black explorers, black labor, black insurrections, and black soldiers. Other chapters recited the role of Negro Americans in heading America toward something resembling a democracy; "how the black woman . . . united two great human races" and "helped lift herself and all women to economic independence"; related how Negroes had contributed to American folk music, art, and literature; and told "how the fine sweet spirit of black folk, despite superstition and passion, has breathed the soul of humanity and forgiveness into the formalism and cant of American religion." While the tone of the book is assertive, compared to *Darkwater* it is far less grim a recital of black horrors, and less hostile to white society though still insistent upon its essential and cruel bigotry. Du Bois's thesis is that "dramatically the Negro is the central thread of American history," providing the labor that built and preserved the nation, becoming a social force around which much of the nation's political and military history revolved, and making a gift of its particular spirit to help create what is most distinctive in the American democratic experiment and in various American art forms. "America as we know it," Du Bois declares, "would have been impossible" without the Negro. At the same time he is careful to quote with complete approval the words of the Negro minister J. W. C. Pennington spoken before the Civil War: "The colored population of the United States has no destiny separate from that of the nation in which they form an integral part. Our destiny is bound up with that of America. Her ship is ours; her pilot is ours."

Du Bois also laments the failure of the best of the plantation class to align themselves with their former slaves following the Civil War to build up "a political party or even parties of the best of the black and white South." Instead, he concludes, the control of the South passed into the hands of the "newer town capitalists" and Northern industrialists who pitted Negro and white laborers against each other to produce a land meager in "science, litera-

ture, and art . . . the one region in the civilized world where
sometimes men are publically burned alive at the stake." Thus Du
Bois suggested that almost lost were the possibilities of a white-
black union of which he wanted both his black and white readers
still to be aware, though he also wanted his audience to understand clearly the realities of America's racially divided state, a
segregated society strongly resisting change.

Like much of Du Bois's work the book is not easy to evaluate.
Du Bois was mixed in his own later response to it, stating in *Dusk
of Dawn* that he thought it "basically sound . . . but too hurriedly
done, with several unpardonable errors." Usually his prose in the
essays is good, clear exposition, lacking the evocative power of his
best work but avoiding the bloated ponderousness of his artifi-
cially heightened verbiage. Sometimes his need to recite a great
many facts rapidly leads him into writing choppy, badly organized paragraphs, but most of the information he packs into his
text is smoothly integrated. The historical narratives are never
dull, and are often spiced with memorable quotations such as
General Hunter's reply to superiors who demanded to know
during the Civil War "whether he had enlisted fugitive slaves and
upon what authority?"—to which he replied that "no regiment of
'fugitive slaves' has been, or is being, organized in this department. There is, however, a fine regiment of loyal persons whose
late masters are fugitive rebels." Du Bois also contributes his own
incisive phrasing adding flavor to the narratives: "There was one
thing that the white South feared more than Negro dishonesty,
ignorance, and incompetency," he observes with biting humor
about postbellum Southern attitudes, "and that was Negro honesty, knowledge, and efficiency."

As a book attempting to compensate for the miseducation most
black and white Americans received about Negro history, the
work is successful, for it contains much information effectively
communicated. As a historical narrative with solid proofs and
accurate details, the work has certain deficiencies. Again Du Bois's
research was random and occasionally inexact, and some of his
conjectures dubious, for example, the claim that "the mounds of
the [Indian] Mound Builders" were probably replicas of Negro
forts in Africa. Sometimes his generalities while salutory in noting
real contributions Negroes had made to American culture, are
overstated, such as when he states that Negro folk songs are "the
only American folk music."

Yet much of what Du Bois claimed for the Negro in *The Gifts of Black Folk* accurately related the nature and extent of Negro contributions to American democracy and culture, and constituted a healthy antidote to the appalling lack of such information possessed by many Americans. In emphasizing the significance of the slave and then free black labor force, that the "foundation of America is built on the backs of the [mostly black] manual laborer," Du Bois was stating what few historians before him had stated with such definiteness. Moreover, his insistence that Negroes had made major contributions—often unacknowledged and under frightening circumstances—to the safety and prosperity of the democratic state, recognized a valid and unpaid debt owed Negro Americans. The "Black Mammy . . . 'drab and dirty drudge or dark and gentle lady . . . [who] played her part in the uplift of the South"; "the Negro woman . . . the protagonist in the fight for an economically independent womanhood in modern countries"; black inventors such as Jan E. Matzlinger who revolutionized the shoe industry with a machine ironically called "the Niggerhead machine"; the "real grandeur of" black religion (though Du Bois did not like its "influences of a primitive sort and customs that belong to the unlettered childhood of civilization rather than to the thinking adult life of civilization"); all these and others offered gifts often unrecognized by the white society that continued to assert and legislate its own superiority.

Du Bois is at his most effective when dealing with areas where he had himself performed considerable research. His chapters touching upon the Civil War and Reconstruction presage the great achievement he would later make in these periods. The moral fiber of the Negro emerges strongly in these pages, for Du Bois documents and narrates how Negroes fought for the right to fight for their freedom in the Civil War at a time when some of the most vicious treatment they would receive—from being spat upon to being lynched—would occur to them in the North, and not infrequently when they were in uniform. He shows that situation was repeated during World War I, when Negroes also had to campaign for the right to bear arms, and then were still discriminated against in the army.

Yet his chapters on the folk song are not as expressive as his earlier treatment in *The Souls of Black Folk*, and his comments on major black writers such as Paul Laurence Dunbar lack depth. Most curiously, he failed to write about the artistic explosion going

on about him and in which he was participating—the so-called
Harlem Renaissance—declaring instead that "the time has not yet
come for the great development of American Negro literature."
Some of Du Bois's racial conjectures now appear themselves tinged
with traditional, stereotyped attitudes. "The peculiar spiritual
quality which the Negro has injected into American life," he says,
sounding very much like a (well-meaning) white intellectual, is
characterized by "a certain spiritual joyousness; a sensuous,
tropical love of life . . . a slow and dreamful conception of the
universe, a drawling and slurring of speech," none of which Du
Bois appeared to possess, "and intense sensitiveness to spiritual
values." But here and elsewhere in the book he was at least
presenting a positive image of blackness, making this image up
from details that white racists either had never seen or from what
they had contorted into something ugly and inferior. While
neither as solid historically nor as fervently compelling as some of
his earlier major works, *The Gift of Black Folk* was a competently
written corrective to the standard white version of American
history.

VI   *A Faerie Queen Reigneth in Harlem:* Dark Princess

Du Bois's next major work was written at the height of the
Harlem Renaissance. It appeared after a particularly eventful
two-year period for Du Bois during which he traveled to Liberia
and Russia, founded the Krigwa Players in Harlem, and attended
the Fourth Pan-African Congress in New York. *Dark Princess*
(1928) could be termed an early third-world novel though most of
the oppressed third-worlders seem overly cultured, well-heeled
snobs—certainly not the victimized proletariat—and strangely
ignorant about black American life. In *Dusk of Dawn* he termed it
his favorite work, but critics have been nearly unanimous in
calling the novel a failure. In *Negro Voices in American Fiction*,
for example, Hugh Gloster stated that the work suggested Du Bois
was "more of a propagandist than a realistic painter of folk and
the social scene." Julius Lester declared that the novel suffered
from "romantic unrealism" while Leslie Lacy complained of Du
Bois's "irrelevant references" in the book to a variety of modernist
painters and writers, and of "static characterization." Arnold
Rampersad charitably admits that *Dark Princess* was not "thoroughly successful in its objectives," but added that it defined "some

of Du Bois' most ambitious thoughts during the middle passage of his life."

The book first relates the life and early hard times of Matthew Towns, a victim of racism in America that prevents him from gaining his degree in obstetrics, who then wanders around Paris where he stumbles upon an organization of "colored" elite headed by the beautiful and mysterious woman who at the book's end becomes Matthew's bride. She is the dark princess of the book's title, and by marrying her Matthew achieves a kind of secular apotheosis as Majarajah of the mythical Indian kingdom of Bwodophur.

Du Bois surrenders in the book to the sentimental strain always lurking beneath the austere surface of his wintry prose and puritanic life-style. The language he employs is often overripe. The princess, "carefully groomed from her purple hair to her slim toe-tips . . . luminous" in the "radiance of her young beauty" is insubstantial and ridiculously exotic. Matthew is dull and like all the book's characters manipulated by Du Bois into speech and actions that are often unrealistic. Some of the book's minor characters are well sketched if not fully developed, especially the nervy, quick-witted, shrewd Sara Andrews, a talented driving black woman who makes Matthew seem rather sappy, and pragmatic, foxy Sammy Scott, a likable if totally crooked political hustler. But melodramatic behavior and dialogue overwhelm what faint interest might reside in the few scenes of black political life that are realistically depicted: the book even contains stolen crown jewels worth millions. Matthew solemnly explains that his "mother, now many years a widow, farmed her little forty acres to educate me, her only child," exclaims another time, "Bosh . . . that was pure poppycock," and once a black prostitute calls to him with the hoary line "hello, Big Boy."

Students of Du Bois if not students of the novel will find some interest in the book, which Harold Isaacs noted contains many of Du Bois's "thoughts and fantasies."[15] Some biographical details tie Matthew to Du Bois, including his light skin and mixed blood, his worship of his mother and the near nonexistence of his father, his triumphant march through various schools, his latent violence ("there was murder in his mind—murder, riot, and arson") restrained by doubt that violence is efficacious, his hostility toward the black church, and his nebulous socialism. Some fancy ideological footwork by the princess attempts to resolve what would always be a conflict between Du Bois's developing belief in the genius inherent in the masses and the intellectual elitism that so often complemented his proletariat sympathies. The princess writes a letter to Matthew telling him that the "oligarchy" Matthew fears will necessarily control the emancipation of the industrial world is not incompatible with the democratic way, for the "oligarchy as you conceive it is not the antithesis of democracy—it is democracy, if only the selection of the oligarchs is just and true." Thus she and Matthew are free to rule the common folk.

Matthew belongs to a tradition of heroes in Du Bois's work starting with Bles in *The Quest of the Silver Fleece* and culminating with Mansart in the "Black Flame" trilogy who rise from humble origins to become exceptional men, the new black quality, far removed from the daily patterns of life of most black Americans. *Dark Princess* is another of Du Bois's attempts to convince black and white America and "colored" races around the world that racial injustice can and should be overcome, but it is also a book that seems a snob's view of what a just life for the races of mankind might be like. What value the book possesses in terms of revealing Du Bois's mind is muffled by bad writing such as the princess's heated declaration that "there shall be no fire tonight, save in our twined bodies and in our flaming hearts." The book is Du Bois at his worst, far inferior to his excellent journalism of the period, demonstrating not even a hint of the powerful, sustained, scholarly effort to which he would soon return.

CHAPTER 5

A New Life

FOLLOWING his resignation from the NAACP, Du Bois would never again occupy the commanding position for commenting on racial affairs that his editorship of the *Crisis* afforded him. However, the experiences he crammed into the long, last quarter of his career would have by themselves justified calling his life fulfilled by any standards save perhaps his own, which were impossibly high. Even the public setbacks he met he would ultimately turn into triumphs though he might not have recognized them immediately as such. The private, personal losses he endured these years were lived through and partly compensated for by new joys and new loves.

In 1934 his old friend John Hope, president of Atlanta University, offered Du Bois the chance to become once again a professor at Atlanta and chairman of the Department of Sociology. So one year beyond the ordinary retirement age of sixty-five, Du Bois started out again in Atlanta with impressive plans for continuing his lifelong struggle for black equality. His aims were to write more about the Negro, to establish a scholarly journal concerned with race, and once again to institute some program that would systematically study what he called the "Negro Problem." Prevented from achieving all he wanted because of Hope's death in 1936 and the subsequent lack of adequate administrative support for his plans, but thwarted too by his own testy personality and by the sheer magnitude (as always) of his aspirations, Du Bois nonetheless accomplished much until he was—surprisingly to him—forced to retire in 1944.

His major publications after his severance from the NAACP were varied in subject and approach and uneven in performance, but considered as a group demonstrate once again the remarkable range of Du Bois's interest in black affairs. *Black Reconstruction*

(1935) was a brilliant scholarly polemic proving that it was white America which failed to take advantage of the possibilities of black reconstruction, not black America. *Black Folk Then and Now* (1937) expanded upon and extended some of the materials originally used in *The Negro*, to show the rich history of the race in Africa and America. *Dusk of Dawn* (1940) continued the personal and racial autobiography Du Bois had begun in *Souls of Black Folk*. The magazine *Phylon* that he helped found in 1940 was and is one of the most respected in its field, an excellent periodical focusing mainly upon the sociological investigation of racial issues. His attempt to start a new series of conferences concerned with racial matters began well, in April 1941, but succumbed when he was retired from Atlanta in 1944, thus aborting his plan to have black land-grant colleges work together to run yearly programs investigating black life, especially aspects of the black economy. But his failure to achieve this one goal should not obscure the value of the work he completed so successfully during this period, including at least one undoubted masterpiece, *Black Reconstruction*.

I   *A Black Marxist Historian:* Black Reconstruction

In the midst of his country's deepest depression, during a time of national breakdown and personal turbulence, Du Bois wrote *Black Reconstruction in America*, perhaps his most impressive work. Lacking the tightness and unity of *The Suppression of the African Slave-Trade*, the great fervid shocks of *The Souls of Black Folk*, the clarity and coherence of *The Philadelphia Negro*, *Black Reconstruction* is at times an outraged but nearly always powerfully and painfully revealing investigation of how America treated the Negro and was in turn treated by him during that most critical and tragic period of Negro history which followed upon the joy of black emancipation in 1863.

Du Bois had long been interested in the subject. As early as September 1902 he had received a request for a talk in Boston on the black side of Reconstruction from Monroe Trotter. In July 1909, J. R. L. Diggs, president of the Virginia Theological Seminary in Lynchburg and one of the founders of the Niagara Movement, sent Du Bois a letter asking him to contribute to a projected series of books that would counteract works generally hostile to the Negro's role during the period. And he had delivered a talk in December 1909 at the American Historical Association on the topic, "Reconstruction and its Benefits." In 1930 he started concentrated work on his study which he did not finish practically until the day it was published in 1935, for almost until that time he labored hard to verify the many citations he had compiled over the years, which he at one time had lost. Herbert Aptheker reports that he revised the massive volume four or five times, cutting about 250 pages during the summer of 1934.[1] He worked especially hard to make it, in Du Bois's terms, a "piece of literature" and not something resembling "a Ph.D. thesis, well documented: but with far too many figures."[2] He produced a volume culminating his academic career of reconstructing the image of blacks in history. At seventy-seven he created a work rich in charaterization, full to the brim with relevant detail, cool, controlled, and vibrant, a book that, as he wrote to F. P. Keppel, a representative of the Carnegie Fund, might not sell but "can never be ignored."

Du Bois seems to have viewed slavery as a nearly totally disastrous system, an absolutely shameful episode that contributed little to the advancement of black culture save isolated elements such as the "sorrow songs" and the periodic displays of courage by insurgent blacks. He wrote comparatively little on the subject (excluding the trade in slaves). Reconstruction was a topic more amenable to him, for by accurately portraying the realities of the black response to the awesome and unfair challenge forced upon them by emancipation, he could correct the impression set forth by so many white historians that the Negroes displayed only their innate inferiority when given a chance to determine their political destiny. He could instead present the truth, which for him was their remarkable courage and unsuspected wisdom when given the rare opportunity to help direct (though never to control) their own lives.

Du Bois believed that "the whole history of Reconstruction has with few exceptions been written by passionate believers in the inferiority of the Negro." At the outset of his investigation Du Bois attempted to offset this racist theory with an assumption of his own written with justifiable bitterness: "I am going to tell this story as though Negroes were ordinary human beings, realizing that this attitude will from the first seriously curtail my audience." But there is no pervasive tone of bitterness in the book, for mainly Du Bois presents his facts from the perspective of one watching a terrible tragedy work itself out relentlessly, the downfall of a near-democracy given the chance to achieve true democracy through establishing a just society for black and white, poor and rich, but doomed through its continued embrace of exploitive capitalism and irrational, racial prejudice. The two-fold movement the book describes toward a true democracy propelled by a "normal black working class . . . successful to an unusual degree, despite all disappointment and failure," and the contrary pull away from democracy toward what is sometimes called today the power elite, provide Du Bois with a dramatically tense historical backdrop against which he shows individuals and classes playing out their at once depressing and sometimes exhilarating struggles.

Du Bois first describes the nature and historic performance of the classes involved in the fight for democracy, classes distinguished partly by race and partly by economic interest. Chief among these protagonists is the black worker. Black labor, he writes in the first chapter, "became the foundation stone not only of the Southern social structure, but of Northern manufacture and commerce, of the English factory system, of European commerce; . . . new cities were built on a world-wide scale" because of the new wealth black labor made available, yet the black laborer under the slave system remained politically powerless. The fate of black labor, Du Bois declares, would determine "what were to be the limits of democratic control in the United States," for until black labor was made free *and equal*, democracy would be a sham.

Next Du Bois describes the life of the white laborer especially as that life intersected with the life of the black worker. Both a black historian and Marxist historian, Du Bois divides the white working class into several groups. First were the poor Southern whites whose class interests should have allied them with the black workers, but who were constantly being manipulated into conflict with the blacks. Sometimes their antagonism was rational, particularly that resulting from the unequal contest for manual jobs the slaves were forced to perform more cheaply in terms of the lack of wages paid them. But the poor white hatred of blacks was also fostered by the ruling plantation class as a way of containing the black laborers. Du Bois is sympathetic to the poor whites, whose choices for a new partner in political coalition seemed limited to the planter who had contempt for them, the "carpetbagger Capitalist" the Southern poor whites had just fought, or the Negro whom they had been trained to fear and treat with contempt.

Second, the white workers in the North comprised at least two classes, slum dwellers of negligible political significance (lumpenproletariat, though Du Bois does not use the term) who Du Bois says were often not as well-off as some slaves; and organized or semiorganized labor, frequently opposed to slavery not so much on moral grounds but through fear of competing economically with a slave caste. Northern labor might sometimes support emancipation of slaves but would too often be cold to further support of the freedmen.

For the third class introduced in this epic history, the plantation owners, Du Bois had some sympathy but little respect. This class represented according to Du Bois seven percent of the South's population, ruling five million whites and owning most of the region's four million slaves. He condemns the class for its economic exploitation of blacks, for the sexual chaos it effected in black life by not respecting black women or any established black family relationships, and by spawning and profitting from children born of mixed blood. Furthermore, he attacks the laziness and self-indulgence which, he claims, the planter exhibited before the Civil War when he failed to "break and arrest the growth of this domination of all industry by trade and manufacture. . . . His capitalistic rivals of the North were hard-working, simple-living zealots" and the planter was not. The North effectively controlled the price of the South's staple product, cotton, and all the planter could do to increase profits was to further shave production costs by exploiting black labor. The planter's assumptions became the South's assumptions: the Negro could not work effectively as free labor; the Negro could not be educated; political power given the Negro "would result virtually in the overthrow of civilization." Reinforcing precepts such as these demanded a massive though not always conscious assault upon the black psyche dedicated to keeping the Negro down. Du Bois holds the planters more than any other group responsible for the contemporary South which he characterized as "an abode of ignorance . . . more abysmal than . . . any modern land."

Even so, he recognized the plight of the planters following their devastation during the Civil War and afterward, their land and fields in shambles, their slaves freed, the economic basis of their life shattered. Further, he underscores the critical failure of various segments of what he calls the proletariat (freed Negroes, Southern poor whites, skilled and common labor in the North) to recognize the mutuality of their interests, and mourns the failure

of the abolitionists, whom Du Bois sees as bourgois liberals, to
"realize the plight of the white laborer, especially the semi-skilled
and unskilled worker."

Drawing closer to the events of the Civil War itself, he then
describes what he curiously designated "the General Strike" of black
labor in the South during the war, when blacks increasingly
transferred their services from "a Confederate planter to the
Northern invader," accompanied by the amazingly nonviolent
behavior of other blacks unable or unwilling to leave their Southern
homes. In a chapter dramatically titled "The Coming of the Lord"
he recaptures the excitement of Negroes during the Civil War who
felt their promised land might soon be won. A major theme of this
chapter and a key idea in the book is the important and militant
role blacks played in their own emancipation. According to Du
Bois, the Civil War was fought over slavery whether the participants realized it or not, and the emancipation of slaves was
necessary for the North to win the war. "Negro military labor . . .
[was] indispensable to the Union armies," and Negro soldiers
absolutely necessary to the successful prosecution of the war.

Du Bois skillfully weaves throughout his text actual speeches of
the participants to intensify and illuminate the historic drama he
describes. He wanted history to come alive, and the heated words
of the antagonists often lend vitality to his generalizations and
supporting facts and documents. He gives, for example, General
Phiel's reply to an order that he not arm Negro troops but set them
to work cutting wood instead: Phiel said while he "was willing to
prepare African regiments for the defense of the government
against its assailants . . . I am not willing to become the mere
slave-driver which you propose, having no qualifications in that
way." Du Bois also quotes General Thomas's reply to those who
questioned the efficacy of using black troops in battle: "Gentle-
men," Thomas succinctly declared, "the question is settled: Negroes will fight."

Extending his narrative into the postwar period, Du Bois shows,
in the chapters titled "Looking Forward" and "Looking Backward," how disparate forces in the North combined to exert
pressure to ensure that the white South radically modify its stands
on a number of political and social issues. In the political
skirmishes fought after the war two especially important groups of
power wielders aided Southern Negroes, whose needs were land,
equality under the law, a chance for proper education, and voting

rights (and who after the smoke of Reconstruction cleared received none of these). In the North existed what Du Bois terms the abolition-democracy—liberals and radicals actuated essentially by a desire that justice be afforded the freed blacks; and the evolving Northern industrialism which feared the return of the old planter aristocracy to political power, thus forcing compromise or even defeat upon policies such as the high tariff which protected Northern industry. These two groups watched with apprehension and dismay as immediately following the war, the third force, the reactionary plantation aristocracy, led the South back down old paths, denying the vote, establishing notorious black codes, and returning many of its old rebel leaders to sit in Congress and vote for planter, not industrial or liberal, interests. Thus as Du Bois explained, "a movement which began primarily and sincerely to abolish slavery and insure the Negro's rights, became coupled with a struggle of Northern capitalism to retain control of the government." An amazing mutual interest society was thus created opposing the defeated but apparently unhumbled and unregenerate plantation South. Du Bois communicated the strangeness of this union in an arresting and revealing metaphor: "thus by singular coincidence and for a moment, for the few years of an eternal second in a cycle of a thousand years, the orbits of two widely and utterly dissimilar economic systems coincided and the result was a revolution so vast and portentous that few minds ever fully conceived it." A moment of cosmic significance had arrived but the country would let it slip away without fixing it into permanence. Briefly, money-makers and humanitarians were working together truly to free the Negro and achieve a real democracy. The odd alliance would not last.

Du Bois is careful to point out the devastation wreaked upon the South during the war and afterward, bringing about the anarchic disruption of slave, poor white, and planter existence alike. And he admits the particularly intense disruption—the destruction of material property and the economic losses—the planters sustained. But he notes that their response was to "substitute for the individual ownership of slaves, a new state serfdom of black folk," and that they still felt, in the words of the then Secretary of the Treasury Carl Schurz, that "the Negro exists for the special object of raising cotton, rice, and sugar for the whites."

Much of Du Bois's analysis of the Reconstruction period is essentially though not intensively a Marxist critique of the political forces in conflict and sometimes harmony. For him the plantation South "represented the extreme of reactionary capitalism based upon land and on ownership of labor." The capitalistic industrialists of the North feared the power of this South to curtail profits that it felt depended upon policies such as a "high protective tariff, the validity of the public debt, and the control of the national banks and currency." Although the white South's opposition to Negro rights was partly racist irrationality, "fatal because of the attitude of men's minds rather than because of material loss and disorganization," this "racial and social animosity" was less fundamental an obstruction than the Southern "determination of land and capital to restrict the political power of labor." In the struggle between sectional economic forces, then, the Negro was a pawn which the Industrial North found it necessary to arm with the vote in order to disarm the Southern agrarian plutocracy. Unfortunately, labor in both the South and the North failed to acknowledge the commonality of their interests in this battle of capitalistic giants.

While the critique of Reconstruction politics deals basically with the movements, in conflict or tandem, of economically or socially rooted forces, of bodies of men gathered together or against each other as a result of historical powers far removed from individual control, Du Bois's analysis gains dramatic drive and impact by cutting away ideological complexities and virtually ignoring splinter conflicts. With great craft he treats these vast historical movements as though they were animated agencies. He puts humanity back into the abstract force he deals with and weaves these forces incessantly through history like characters in an epic. Heroic individuals perform important roles in Du Bois's dramatic scene and further prevent his analysis from becoming the dehumanized working out of some inevitable but uninteresting historic equation.

Du Bois's long-time hero Wendell Phillips is one such character appearing periodically with clear sight and flashing rhetoric. Frederick Douglass, a man of incomparable integrity and wisdom, emerges as a choral commentator, pointing out the fraudulence of the Fourth of July as a day of independence for the Negro, calling for black men to once again manifest what he considered their inherent right to American citizenship by joining the Northern Army, militantly refusing to leave a racially bigoted labor convention to which he had been legitimately elected.

President Lincoln is a more central character in the drama than Douglass, but in some ways more distant a figure too than the ex-slave. God-like in his separation from the men around him but surely no all-seeing, all-knowing divinity, Lincoln as described by Du Bois is a compassionate man slowly becoming educated into the politics of equality—a man similar to Frederick Douglass's Lincoln as described in Douglass's autobiography: a great man and a great president, but a great white president nonetheless, limited by his (compassionate) white man's perspective on black needs and abilities.

Greater champions for black rights than Lincoln, more heroically involved as Du Bois depicts them in the attempt to grant black folk the same opportunities as whites, are senators Charles Sumner and Thaddeus Stevens. Doughty Sumner, thundering his orations for black equality, "one of the finest examples of New England culture and American courage," agitating for Negro suffrage, trying unsuccessfully to hector a radical civil rights bill through Congress, and wearing down his heavy body through incessant attack upon the old, immoral citadel of prejudice he saw in the South; Stevens, the smoother but equally dedicated politician, one of the great "leaders of the common people," older than Sumner and often sick, "more realistic" than Sumner as he tried to engineer bills through Congress through astute manipulation of men and through compromise, but perhaps even more than Sumner hostile to the consciousless white South—the speeches and maneuverings of each man are threaded through the historical narrative like guidelines by which to follow the best thought of the North. The acts of these men as they approached death become like acts of martyrs in what Du Bois considered democracy's tragic doom. Sumner died in 1874 attended by Frederick Douglass and two other black men at his bedside, pleading to them hoarsely, "you must take care of . . . my bill, the civil rights bill." Stevens died in August 1868 not long after praying with "two colored clergymen," and was "buried in a colored graveyard" under a stone carved with the inscription he had ordered: "I repose in this quiet and secluded spot, not from any natural perference for solitude, but finding other cemetaries limited as to race by charter rules. . . ."

Du Bois gives few opposition names much weight, presenting the enemy rather as a mass with few memorable faces. Andrew Johnson, however, breaks the ranks from the mob and appears as a representative figure from the forces of reaction and moral obtuseness. Du Bois treats Johnson as the embodiment of poor white values, a president by accident whose ruling passions were a hatred of the planter aristocracy that actually masked a fear and even admiration of them, and a contempt for blacks unalloyed by any mitigating feeling for their predicament. The Negroes needed a Moses, Du Bois quotes Sumner as remarking, but in Johnson they found only another Pharaoh!

In Du Bois's vast prose mural of statistics, events, and characters, one figure towers over all in terms of its complexity, power, and humanity: the spirit of black folk. Sometimes this spirit is manifest in a particular body such as that of Douglass, or Jonathan Gibbs (one-time superintendent of education in Florida) or Hiram Revels (senator from Mississippi) or Francis L. Cardozo (treasurer of South Carolina). Often that spirit was revealed in the undifferentiated masses of black men and women who walked away from slavery and toward an unknown freedom before and during the war, or who fought in the war even while they were spat upon or prejudicially treated in the North (for example, receiving less pay than white soldiers), or who tried to vote after the war. So frequently vilified in their own time and since by white demagogues and historians, these folk are depicted in *Black Reconstruction* as sometimes ignorant, occasionally venal, but generally demonstrating amazing folk-wisdom and charitability and tenacity in their struggle for right in an often unresponsive or hostile land.

The nature of the struggle described state by state constitutes the bulk of Du Bois's book, which is replete with facts and figures that statistically depict the brief flowering and ruthless uprooting of black rights in the South. Although this section of the book is lengthy and highly detailed, and though Du Bois notes how in various states the intricacies of Reconstruction produced disparate, complex, and distinctive configurations, he also demonstrates that overall a clear pattern of black response and reactionary Southern counterresponse existed. Whether the state were one with a black majority such as Mississippi or a state where blacks were a minority such as Virginia, whether the state emerged from the war essentially as it had entered such as Florida or bankrupt such as North Carolina or devastated such as Georgia, Du Bois shows that a composite history could be written portraying the separate states as a single entity with a core of common experiences.

Typically, Southern newspapers and politicians would attack with virulent racism the first postwar attempts in Southern states at black political participation. A constitutional convention called in North Carolina was called in the press an example of "Ethiopian minstrelsy, Ham radicalism in its glory," its black members referred to by a white politician as "adventurers, manikens, and gibbering Africans." A common assumption often expressed publicly and in print was that "the Negro is utterly unfitted to exercise the highest function of a citizen . . . [is from an] ignorant and depraved race . . . [and has been] placed in power and influence above the virtuous, the educated, and the refined."

Violence and terror were systematically applied as techniques to destroy black aspirations. One Northern general reported that during an eighteen-month period ending 30 June 1867, 197 radically instigated murders were committed in North and South Carolina by whites. In six months of 1871 in nine counties of South Carolina, according to one report, thirty-five black men were murdered by the Ku Klux Klan. In 1866, black delegates called to a duly convened constitutional revision convention in Louisiana were surrounded by armed whites who killed, in what contemporary accounts termed "an absolute massacre," from thirty-eight to forty-eight Negroes.

Ordinarily in the defeated rebel states white leaders would call for the constitutional conventions necessary for a state to gain readmission to the Union. These conventions typically (and often grudgingly) admitted that Negroes were no longer slaves, but many failed to pass the proposed Fourteenth Amendment which declared that states would be apportioned representation in Congress only on the basis of the total male population that was allowed to vote, a measure calculated to ensure either that black men could vote, or that their number (if they were not allowed to vote) could not be counted in determining representation. Often, as the first General Assembly in North Carolina determined, only whites were to be permitted to vote and hold office. "Black Codes" were passed limiting the right of Negroes to move from one job to another or even from one locale to another, and permitting their testimony in court only in cases concerning other Negroes. In light of such Southern intransigence once again denying basic rights to Negroes and reinstalling the agrarian aristocracy on the throne of political power, Northern abolitionists and industrialists according to Du Bois were forced to combine to ensure that blacks could vote and participate in government. Thus for a time the South was treated like the defeated province it was and a federal government with its army attempted to guarantee a new, liberalized political order that was also highly advantageous to Northern industrialist goals.

This new order which for the first time in American history allowed blacks to help determine their region's destiny, had been viewed too frequently, according to Du Bois, as a time of disorder and unparalleled corruption in the South, caused by the blacks who had been suddenly thrust into a position of political leadership by Northerners manipulating them behind the scenes. Du Bois vigorously and with great masses of documentary evidence attacked all aspects of this myth which was, he said, promulgated for essentially two reasons: it reinforced racial stereotypes of black inferiority, and it reaffirmed class biases. Again, he operated as a black Marxist historian. "Poor men," he pointed out, "were ruling and taxing rich men. And this was the chief reason that ridicule and scorn and crazy anger were poured upon the government."

Carefully and with patiently presented factual detail, Du Bois tried to dispel the Reconstruction myth. He noted that at no time in any Southern state did blacks have a majority in both legislative houses. Even in South Carolina with is preponderance of black voters, whites always held a majority in the Senate. He noted that given the opportunity to disfranchise whites, the blacks were loath to do so, so that the total of whites voting in elections remained relatively constant with prewar levels. Further, he quoted speeches of black legislators who refused to disfranchise the ex-Confederates whom Northern radicals would have prohibited from voting. He pointed out that state administrations and civil services remained overwhelmingly white. He demonstrated that the new "black" constitutions were usually far better instruments for the commonweal than were the old, providing as they so frequently did for improved public school systems and for other humanitarian social services aiding especially the poor but black and white alike.

He answered in a number of ways the charges that black legislators caused monstrous debt throughout the South through their ignorance and greed. First, he reiterated that blacks never controlled any state government. Next, he showed that many increased expenditures resulted from wise social measures instituted by blacks who, for example, tried to do what the old, white governments never attempted, namely, guarantee a public school education for all citizens. And he repeated that the improved social services so frequently sought by Negro politicians were intended for all citizens, not merely black ones. The charge of corruption he confronts head-on, admitting that during this age of American governments preeminent for their political bamboo-zling, the time of Boss Tweed and his gigantic rake-offs and kickbacks in New York City, of the notoriously corrupt Grant administration, some blacks in local governments accepted bribes. But, he states, "only in so far as they represented ignorance and poverty and were thus peculiarly susceptible to petty bribery" should they be held accountable for their relatively meager participation in the postbellum plundering. Most of the payments and profits went to whites, to Northern promoters and Southern white administrators. To the charges of black wastefulness and extravagance, he tersely replied, "somehow, I have more respect for the gold spittoons of freed Negro lawmakers in 1872, than for the chaste elegance of the colonial mansions of slave drivers in 1860." Thus he attacked the Reconstruction myth with his wit and verbal skill as well as with his statistics.

He concludes from his studies that against great odds the newly freed and barely franchised blacks compiled an "excellent record" during their fleeting and tenuous period of political participation. He convincingly demonstrated that black legislators typically sought more rights for black people and for poor people, not fewer rights for whites, except rights that were not rights at all but rather class or race privileges. By judicious use of quotation he permitted the black legislators to voice their own ideas and to demonstrate their concern for the total community in perceptive and eloquent words, and contrasts their measured and reasonable remarks with the strident claims of such opposition spokesmen as the military leader and writer Albert Pike who declared that Negro suffrage would bring about "a hell on earth, a hideous, horrid pandemonium filled with all the devils of vice, crime, pauperism, corrupt violence, political debauchery, [and] social anarchy."

Du Bois shows that ultimately the shaky power base supporting black democracy in the South eroded or was blasted away by white force, fraud, moral enervation, and political connivance. What he terms the "counter-revolution of property" in the North, instituting a "trusteeship of capital" based upon the common

political goals of the great corporations, found it expedient and
profitable to foster white capitalist aims in the South and at the
same time assimilate the white entrepreneural class into its own
oligarchy which as always had no place in its power structure for
the poor or for the black. And so the democratic experiment
ended, but not before it had achieved unparalleled reform in the
South: instituting an extended public school system, opening the
jury and ballot box to thousands of blacks and whites previously
excluded, appropriating large sums of money for public works
needed by the many and not just the few, and abrogating no man's
or woman's just rights.

II   A Black Marxist Writer

Du Bois was a historian who well understood the need to drive
home his ideas in an effective prose style, especially the need in
such a lengthy and fact-filled book as *Black Reconstruction*. He
graced the book with imaginative touches few other academics
would have employed. Each chapter, for example, concludes with
an appropriate poem, some of which are not only quite powerful
in themselves, but also historically revealing. Chapter 7, "Looking
Forward," deals with black aspirations following the war. The
poem appended to the chapter, written by Du Bois's protégé the
black writer Jessie Fauset, depicts black Americans who "clutch-
ing our birthright, fight with faces set, / Still visioning the stars!"
Fauset's lines declare that the fight for freedom was not over yet,
that freedom was still sought. The poems also reveal Du Bois's
catholicity of taste, and include passages by Oscar Wilde, Schiller,
and Shelley.

Stylistically the book is varied. Many of the facts and details are
stated with no rhetorical flourishes whatsoever, in clear if unspectacular prose. Du Bois often employs a simple style to deal with
complex and emotion-laden matters, a plain style that travels
straight as a nail to the core of subjects not easy to write about
effectively. He is especially adept at evoking through basic images
the emotional context of certain situations. "The propaganda
which made the abolition movement terribly real," he writes,
"was the fugitive slave—the piece of intelligent humanity who
could say: I have been owned like an ox. I stole my own body and
now I am hunted by law and lash to be made an ox again."
Another time he coolly expressed the real pain of slavery using

simple phrasing and simple yet magnetic cadences: "It was in part psychological, the enforced personal feeling of inferiority, the calling of another master; the standing with hat in hand. It was the helplessness. It was the defenselessness of family life." The simple middle image, the "standing with hat in hand," seems especially poignant, yet not sentimental.

There are passages, too, written in Du Bois's familiar high style, more controlled here and more sparingly used than in his novels. He uses a familiar image and familiar abstractions to describe black life where "beneath the Veil lay right and wrong, vengeance and love, and sometimes throwing aside the veil, a soul of sweet Beauty and Truth stood revealed." While occasionally Du Bois indulged in a self-consciously arty style, he could also obtain stunning effects by juxtaposing it to more soberly written factual passages, as he does when discussing the struggle of white workers to achieve a measure of democracy in America's fertile land. He writes first as any informed historian might of white labor's troubled experiences in the new world, mentioning specific problems and movements, and then adds shockingly—as few historians would—a strange but arresting image, attempting to communicate the disturbance forced black labor introduced into the lives of whites: "And then some unjust God leaned, laughing, over the ramparts of heaven and dropped a black man in the midst." His cosmic irony here lights up the problem he has been describing and forces the reader to examine Du Bois's subject from this new light.

Always careful to explain broad social movements, to set down and examine speeches, to marshal statistics, he seems also determined to reach that level of history beyond the recitation or explication of facts, where often only creative historians aspire. He painstakingly follows the intricate politics of emancipation, showing, for example, Lincoln's wavering attitude toward it, but when he tells of its declaration his prose erupts like the message of a jubilant black minister, capturing the passion that must have been felt by freed blacks. "There was a joy in the South," he begins slowly. "It rose like perfume—like a prayer," he adds moving toward his climax. "Men stood quivering. Slim dark girls, wild and beautiful with wrinkled hair, wept silently; young women, black, tawny, white and golden, lifted shivering hands, and old and broken mothers black and gray, raised great voices and shouted to God across the fields, and up to the rocks and the mountains." The passage begins with the language of exhaltation, bursts into the thunder of "shouted to God," and then simply and effectively concludes with language reminiscent of the sorrow songs (and the Bible), describing the landscape of deliverance. Sometimes his fervor slides into anger at human cupidity and hatefulness, as when he chronicles the fate of Southerners who know that their proper enemy was intolerance and not the Negro, who "were soon threatened into silence; and there prevailed a bitter hatred and cry for vengeance from people who could not brook defeat because they had been used to victory, and had the slave-born habit of arrogance." But his wrath is nearly always controlled by a disciplined prose style and tempered by his awareness that vicious people are themselves victims of social and political forces they have not set into motion and which they are rarely capable of stopping. His attitude seems often similar to the sympathetic response of the ex-slaves whose angry and eloquent and surprisingly forgiving words he often quotes.

Du Bois was not a perfect writer and never wrote a perfect book, and certainly some deficiencies are apparent in his narrative. While the overall organization of his book is excellent, some of the later chapters are clumsily structured internally, and he does not always include proper transitions internal to his chapters. Since he did almost no original research himself, he was again at the mercy of his sources, not all of which are equally reliable. Of course, in such a large book crammed with much information, some details are incorrect. He wrongly identifies Sierra Leone as a Bantu region, confuses General William T. Sherman with General Thomas W. Sherman, and misspells Martin Delany's name consistently. His zealous Marxism, while providing him with an excellent analytic tool with which to examine the Reconstruction, also forces him into a few dubious judgments—or more likely his incorrect application of Marxism leads to the errors. He claims that what he terms the dictatorship of black labor constituted "one of the most extraordinary experiments of Marxism before the Russian Revolution" but the entire thrust of his text shows that black labor never attained a dictatorship, and that such powers it possessed were directed mainly toward capitalistic enterprise. His explanation of why American socialists helped so little with the plight of black labor throughout the Reconstruction period— because the abolition movement was based on "mawkish senti-

mentality, and not on the demands of the [white] workers"—
seems a weak apology. His use of the term "strike" to describe the
response of black plantation workers during the war seems highly
dubious.

But the flaws the book possesses do not destroy its worth as a
powerfully written, perceptive analysis of the political and economic realities—and the emotional climate—that brought about
and finally terminated black Reconstruction in the South. Possibly
some of its particular claims are excessive, but its perspective is
well employed, its theses fully documented, its insights persua-
sively corrective of many earlier held popular and academic
views. It is perhaps overly long, but its scope is great and its
revisionist task vast. The eminent contemporary historian of the
South, T. Harry Williams, has stated that while he could not
agree with all that the book suggests about Reconstruction in the
South—for example, he doubted the abolitionist-democrats were
as significant as Du Bois claimed in bringing about Reconstruction
policies—"in some respects he [Du Bois] got closer to the truth of
Reconstruction than any other writer."[3]

Black Reconstruction was the most creative product of Du Bois's
maturity, written with hope during a time of national breakdown.
Although the book specifically concerns the Reconstruction period
when Negroes were exploited by white Americans and then
deserted "shamelessly," Du Bois makes clear that he is writing
about any attempt by a people—in this instance the black workers
and their families and elected representatives—to exercise domin-
ion over their own lives to establish a just society. In this dramatic
effort, he says, "there is no villain, no idiot, no saint." There are
only men and women some of whom act justly and some of whom
do not. His story, he says, is also the story of people deprived of
rights and attacked by fellowmen "in Africa . . . in India . . . in
China . . . in Alabama," in twentieth-century America. He
despairs that this is what history looks like, but declares throughout the book that this kind of history need not be, that exploitation
and oppression are inevitably self-defeating. In the energy and
skill shown by the ex-slaves during Reconstruction, working
against terrible and unfair odds, and in the energy and skill of Du
Bois's retelling of their story and in his unquenchable search for
justice for all peoples, reside proof, perhaps, that Du Bois's hopes
for humanity were justified.

III   *Twilight of a Leader*: Dusk of Dawn

Dusk of Dawn (1940) is the third work in Du Bois's unique series of racial biographies or autobiographies and, like *Black Reconstruction*, showed the aging but still vital and contentious spokesman for human liberation refusing to submit to the waning decade's frequent mood of defeat, and instead reinforcing its occasional surge toward hope. In his prefatory "Apology" Du Bois says that his book records "dimly but consciously that subtle sense of coming day which one feels of early mornings even when mist and murk hang low." *Souls of the Black Folk*, he notes, had been a "cry at midnight thick within the veil, when none rightly knew the coming day," and *Darkwater* "an exposition and militant challenge, defiant with dogged hope." *Dusk of Dawn* is the most optimistic of the racial biographies, almost cheery in parts, and at the same time the most restricted in subject and tone. It is less experimental in form, smoother and more coherent in its organization, and contains fewer emotional and literary peaks and valleys than its predecessors. Its view of Du Bois's childhood and early maturity is less ecstatic and sad than *The Souls of Black Folk* had suggested, its racial investigations less bitter than those of *Darkwater*. *Dusk of Dawn* seems the somewhat mellowed work of a man old in years but still questing for solutions to the problems of the black, poor, and powerless.

Du Bois is aware throughout the book that while his life was proceeding along its long, winding, and yet clearly directed path, the world around him was undergoing vast changes, even as it was in many terrible ways remaining the same. Born just after the Civil War and writing on the eve of America's entrance into World War II, Du Bois states that his life is significant chiefly because "it was part of a Problem," in fact, the "central problem" of America and the "future world," namely, racial and social injustice. The concurrently personal and universal perspective of his point of view here pervades the book and permits Du Bois to shift smoothly from telling about his own public life to describing the world conditions surrounding him, though he omits narrating most events of his private life during these years. His public record is clear, his private existence simply absent. He says what he thinks about public events or about other Negro figures such as Booker T. Washington (he respects him but considers him still the wrongheaded and somewhat devious operator of the "Tuskeegee Machine"), and Marcus Garvey (whom he thinks sincere but the author of a "crazy" and "grandiose and bombastic scheme"). But what he thought about himself quietly at night, or about his personal relations with his family he does not say. In *Dusk of Dawn* Du Bois fashions a public memoir recollecting his public life. The lack of any deep self-analysis is disappointing.

He does examine at length, however, and in a variety of ways, "the chief fact of his life" which was "race." He writes, for example, of the growing and changing awareness of Africa within him, from the time that all he knew of it was a meaningless song handed down in his family, to the periods when he was instrumental in organizing Pan-African conferences. He again rehearses the story of his childhood, but perhaps because so much of the book is emotion recollected in tranquillity he introduces nothing new of an intensely revealing nature. The information he supplies about his ancestors, more carefully worked out into a genealogical tree than in the other racial biographies, demonstrates again the pride he felt in his family, but except in its more detailed picture of the racial and ethnic mix that produced him, offers nothing new to help explain the complex man he became. Great Barrington still resembles one of the snug villages Washington Irving enjoyed describing (or inventing), "shut in by its mountains and provincialism but . . . a beautiful place, a little New England town nestled shyly in its valley with something of Dutch cleanliness and English reticence." His mother, he writes, was brown and small, with lovely eyes, his father still the enigmatic figure who "died in my infancy so that I do not remember him." His prose is clear, simple, direct, but often skims along the surface of what must have been childhood years more troubled sometimes than he cared to admit, years often joyful but that also left scars as they strengthened Du Bois's developing character.

Not all the recollections are as pastorally idyllic as, for example, his memory of his first trip to Africa in 1923. He is completely realistic in describing the strategies he adopted to attack the race problem that dominated his life certainly from the time he attended Fisk. His early assumption had been that cool reason would convince a reasonable but ill-informed world that as human beings, Negroes naturally deserved equitable treatment. Then he came to see that "science alone could" not "settle this matter, but force must come to its aid. . . . with the weapons of truth" and with "the sword of the intrepid . . . with organization in boycott, propaganda," and even "mob frenzy." But then World War I crushed this dream, proving to him that "the color bar could not be broken by a series of immediate assaults," for strongly entrenched economic factors still underlay the idiotic irrationality of racial prejudice. The citadel of injustice would not fall to "sudden assault" but needed a "long seige." Long before World War I, however, Du Bois had been gnawed by the bitter knowledge that impressive monographs portraying the conditions of blacks in America seemed invisible beside the knuckles of the lynched black man displayed in a Georgia grocery store. He mentions but does not dwell on such horrors in *Dusk of Dawn*, though clearly they contributed to his growing feeling as the twentieth century unraveled that his scholar's life was not solving the problem of race that determined his life.

Du Bois offers an informative but mellowed version of his acrid dispute with the NAACP concerning voluntary black segregation, emphasizing that his plan aimed at two targets concurrently: the building up of the black community so that it might be an effective and powerful economic agent in a country dominated by white economic interests, and the ultimate "admission of the colored group to cooperation and incorporation into the white group on the best possible terms." Black schools run by blacks, black hospitals staffed by blacks, black economic cooperatives organized and directed by blacks all involved voluntary segregation, but were, he claimed, forced on Negroes by a white society that permitted little beyond token integration. Better to rule one's own black community with fellow blacks than have it controlled by white power blocks—better immediately for the physical and psychological health of blacks, and better ultimately for the acceptance of blacks in an equitable, multiracial society.

But while the book's dominant direction is toward an integrated society, Du Bois's skepticism sometimes reveals itself, as though occasionally through a relatively hopeful veneer of optimism burst forth his old solid grain of racial pessimism. While he questions the efficacy of black emigration movements he admits that his plans would not "decline frankly to face the possibility of eventual emigration from America" of considerable numbers of Negroes if a suitable place could be found for them to develop in. More cynically, he reminds his black audience that while expulsion from America seemed unlikely for Negroes, "There was no likelihood ten years ago of the Jews being expelled from Germany."

Generally Du Bois avoids this kind of ominous theorizing. Dedicated to Joel Spingarn, the civil libertarian, literary critic, and white man whom Du Bois said touched him more closely than any other, *Dusk of Dawn* treats racial bigotry playfully in several fictionalized debates between Du Bois and white bigots, a rare technique for Du Bois. While the work ignores none of the still depressingly constant problems of black life in America, it manages to maintain a strongly positive attitude toward black ability to endure, toward the "soul of the Negro." Once Du Bois asks, "do you know the two finest things in the industry of the West, finer than factory, shop or ship?" He answers, "the black laborer's Saturday night off" and "laughter . . . the delicious chuckle" that belongs to the black world alone.

Dusk of Dawn does not often concern itself with nights off or black chuckles. In a style that is usually direct and simple, lacking the power of some of his earlier prose but without its inflations, he confronts the economic, racial, and political problems of the day that touched his black life. He explains that he "was not and am not a communist," flatly stating that, although he accepted Marx's economic determinism, he did "not believe in the dogma of inevitable revolution." He vehemently attacks the American Communist party for mishandling and exploiting the Scottsboro case,[4] charging that the party was "tragically wrong" in the methods it foolishly pursued to accomplish its ends which, he suggests, were more party centered than involved with the terribly vulnerable young imprisoned black men. Yet his "Basic American Negro Creed" welcomed "the ultimate triumph of some form of Socialism the world over," and he frankly praised the great accomplishments of the Russian revolutionary regime and claimed that "nothing that Russia has done in war and mass murder exceeds what has been done and is being done by the rest of the civilized world."

At the conclusion of *Dusk of Dawn*, in a chapter headed "Revolution," Du Bois describes his seventieth birthday, a happy celebration arranged for him by his colleagues Ira Reid and Rayford Logan. In a talk he gave at a party he summed up the satisfaction he felt toward his life, spent working at a lifelong task he found always interesting and highly meaningful, and declared how glad he was for the "divine gift of laughter" he possessed and for the "partial Puritanism" that made him never "afraid of life." His words were the words of a man who lived well, "testing every

normal appetite, feasting on sunset, sea and hill, and enjoying
wine, women, and song." Had his life been a moving picture this
would have been a fine scene on which to conclude. But his life
was real and not comprised of cinema images, and amazingly
enough he would live another two fairly productive decades,
through times of international madness, personal disappointment,
and finally, triumph.

CHAPTER 6

Wars and Peace

AFTER his severance from Atlanta in 1944, several black colleges offered Du Bois posts, but he accepted instead a position again with the NAACP. His old adversary Walter White directed from New York what Du Bois considered too slick and conservative an operation, but still he was happy to be closer to the center of black political activity. Since Du Bois thought of himself as an activist and not as the grand old man of civil rights, his second term with the organization was as stormy as, though much briefer than, the first. During World War II he had followed his own unpopular path, declaring, for example, that the German treatment of the Jews was based upon a racial philosophy similar to that practiced by Great Britain and the United States toward the black populations within their empires, and that the British had caused more misery than Hitler's Germany. Thus he remained a controversial figure, although he now lacked the authority he once possessed.

Following the war he continued to speak out for the rights of African peoples (including those in the United States) in books such as *Color and Democracy: Colonies and Peace* (1945), and at personal appearances such as the ones he made in 1945 at the Founding Convention of the United Nations and at the sixth Pan-African Congress in Manchester, England, where he was honored as the "father of Pan-Africanism." In 1947 he edited for the NAACP "An Appeal to the World" to end Jim Crow in America, a plea the federal government clearly found repugnant. In 1948 his worn connection with the NAACP finally snapped when he supported, contrary to the wishes of his employers, the Progressive party candidate for president, Henry Wallace. Again he was without a job, with few savings, and again he plunged headlong and headstrong into the fight for peace.

Du Bois was now eighty years of age. He was more an internationalist than he had ever been, and more a socialist, although he had been both of these since early in the century. He was also more distant from the everyday black world, a drifting away that seemed mutual as Du Bois's interests widened and black America's demands became more specific and urgent, and needful of popular, fresh leadership Du Bois could not provide. Du Bois acknowledged and lamented his partial separation, but typically would not compromise his ideals to achieve a closer union with the people whose recognized spokesman he had been decades before.

His left-wing, internationalist proclivities led him to accept Paul Robeson's request to become an honorary official in 1948 of the Council on African Affairs, a group whose opposition to colonialism in Africa was sufficient to place it on the attorney general's list of subversive organizations. In 1949 he attended peace conferences in Paris and Moscow and was one of the organizers in New York City of a Cultural and Scientific Conference for World Peace. In 1950 he becam chairman of the Peace Information Center and more amazingly enough a candidate for the United States Senate on the American Labor party ticket.

In writing about these years in his *Autobiography*, Du Bois makes clear that he was actuated throughout by a desire to obtain a just life not only for black Americans in America but for all underprivileged Americans dominated by a wealthy and generally white power elite. Increasingly during this period when the nation's leaders were baffled and frustrated by first Russia's and then the new China's rise to power, when American hostility to leftist regimes was intensifying, Du Bois more and more sympathized with foreign and communistic governments he felt offered a better life for society's bottom dogs. His support for these regimes not only made him a target for Red-hunting superpatriots in the federal government, but also decreased his popularity with many black Americans who either did not share his internationalism or who felt that the capitalistic system had more to offer them in the present than what might emerge from its unlikely destruction at some future date. No doubt Du Bois was naive (or blindly hopeful) in many of his assumptions and observations about the virtues of communistic governments whose inner workings and histories he never coldly scrutinized with the same unblinking intensity with which he examined Western racism. At the same time, he had faced for a half century and more certain simple, brutal facts about life in America: when he lived in the South the eminent academician traveled with spare parts, overalls, and mechanic's tools in his car so that he would not have to stop at "cracker" gas stations where he would be just another "nigger." In Manhattan in the late forties, when he traveled to work at the NAACP, he had to carry his own lunch because no restaurant in the area would serve Negroes. His blind Stalinism was sad but should not negate the validity of his still vital attacks upon American corruption. Moreover, the far left provided him increasingly with the kind of intellectual recognition and sympathetic emotional rapport that Du Bois needed and deserved.

His wife of fifty-three years died in February 1950. Their long marriage had not been ideal but her death like the death of any very close friend made the old man lonesome. Then on 8 February 1951 he was indicted by the Justice Department as an officer of the Peace Information Center, for failing to register as an agent for a foreign government.

The Peace Information Center was one of many organizations formed during the late 1940s and early 1950s as a direct result of the dangerously increased hostility between the United States and communist-bloc nations. Responding to what they considered subversive communist acts at home and abroad, various federal agencies started an aggressive campaign to combat what they perceived as an anti-American threat. In 1950 eleven high ranking American Communists were arrested, fined, and jailed, and in 1951 Senator Joseph McCarthy of Wisconsin proclaimed that he possessed a list of 205 government employees who were "members of the Communist Party and who . . . are still working and shaping the policy in the State Department." As the Korean War was proving, perhaps as a self-fulfilling act, the heightened confrontation between Western nations and the communist countries was not simply a battle of words.

According to Du Bois's account in the *Autobiography,* the purpose of the Peace Information Center was "simply to tell the people of the United States what other nations were doing and thinking about the war." That the organization directed reports against the United States is undeniable, that it may have in some way been exploited by individuals whose interests were inimical to those of the United States Government's is quite possible, but that Du Bois was absolutely sincere and acting on his own in condemning American foreign and domestic policy is undoubted: the prickly old man had spent part of his lifetime castigating his country, even while sometimes supporting it. The government's action in arresting, fingerprinting, searching for concealed weapons, and handcuffing the eighty-three-year-old scholar was shameful and mean-spirited, proving once again the validity of Henry David Thoreau's dictum that "the State was half-witted, that it was timid as a lone woman with her silver spoons, and that it did not know its friends from its foes."

Du Bois received some support, but not enough, he felt, from the NAACP and from the black elite who were, he claimed in his *Autobiography*, "not. . . outspoken in my defense." But he was pleased at the "mass support which I gained from the Negroes of the nation." In fact, many of the black intelligentsia demonstrated their continued respect for and faith in the old leader, for example, his academic cohorts Rayford Logan and E. Franklin Frazier, and the alumni of Fisk University.

Traveling around the nation to dramatize his ordeal, which he viewed as part of a greater threat to silence dissent in America, Du Bois was aided considerably by Shirley Graham Du Bois, his second wife, whom he had married on 14 February 1951, two days before his arraignment in Washington. Shirley Graham, herself a writer and civil rights activist, had admired Du Bois since the first time they met in Colorado Springs, Colorado, in 1920. After his first wife's death, she became increasingly important to him, and brought a grace and wit to his life, and a passion that had been lacking before on any intimate level.

After nine months of waiting in agony and considerable expense to Du Bois and the other four white defendants, the trial finally began—and ended almost immediately when the government's charges collapsed of their own shoddy insupportability. The judge ruled that the government had in no way demonstrated its contention that the Peace Information Center was an agent for a foreign principal, and a judgment of acquittal was granted. Du Bois had beaten the government.

I *Final Acclaim*

Throughout the 1950s Du Bois continued to write, mainly articles for good, leftist periodicals such as the *National Guardian* and *Masses and Mainstream*, but also longer works such as his Mansart trilogy *The Black Flame* (1957–1961), and fragments

that would later appear in his *Autobiography*. He lectured around
the country, often with his wife, and taught for a time at the
Thomas Jefferson School in downtown Manhattan until, according to Shirley Graham, the government closed the school. His life
continued to be both extraordinary and uneventful: he spoke at
the graveside of the Rosenbergs, executed for alleged treason on 19
June 1953 after being trapped in the same maelstrom of patriotic
panic and zeal that had for a time sucked Du Bois into its vortex;
often he watched "Perry Mason," his favorite television show,
where the lone man upholding right always triumphed. He
constantly compared the world he entered with the world he was
watching even then change around him. Born when Andrew
Johnson was president, he had lived into the late 1950s when Fidel
Castro was parading his troops into Havana to symbolize the
victory of his Cuban revolution.

He continued to travel, especially throughout Eastern Europe,
Russia, and China, and always in these countries he was honored
by the important leaders of the day. At the age of ninety he was
acclaimed by over two thousand friends and well wishers at a
hotel party in New York City, and the next year he was praised at
another celebration in Peking. Throughout this time the American
government, far from honoring one of its most internationally
revered citizens, badgered Du Bois by making it difficult for him
to obtain a passport to journey overseas. After his 1959 trip to
China it took his passport from him.

His life continued until its very close to be filled with work,
dispute, and cherished pleasures with his wife and a few friends.
At ninety-two spry enough to spring from a divingboard into a
Caribbean lagoon and then swim across to the opposite shore, he
was not fully happy unless politically active. He welcomed the
opportunity to travel once again to Africa in 1960, this time to
Ghana where Kwame Nkrumah was engaged in a controversial
but exciting attempt to establish his new nation as a strong, self-
supporting, modern country. Nkrumah asked Du Bois if he would
take charge of plans to produce an *Encyclopedia Africana* which
would demonstrate to the world in a full and systematic fashion
the richness of African history.

In 1961, Du Bois accepted Nkrumah's offer, for he preferred to end
his days at productive work rather than on the sidelines in America.
His departure from the country was swift for, according to Shirley
Graham, they had received word that if they delayed, new restric-

tions on overseas travel could prevent them from ever leaving the country. Concurrent with departing, Du Bois issued a statement noting his membership in the Communist party of the United States. He who had established his name as a race leader partly by declaring so articulately that he saw himself always as a black man and as an American, now was also a Communist and soon would be an African, for in 1963 he would become a citizen of Ghana.

Julius Lester says of Du Bois's decision to join the party that it "was logical." So was his acceptance of Ghanaian citizenship. Neither decision betrayed earlier ideals, but showed that he had progressed beyond them. In his later years the American Communist party probably offered Du Bois more support than any other political organization in the country. Moreover, he had been a socialist for years and clearly felt that achieving a good and just life for American blacks and for a majority of Americans was impossible under capitalism. He also saw the powerful force for change the new Communist governments could show to the twentieth-century world. He was ripe for a more radical alternative to capitalism than socialism and this is what communism seemed to offer. After a lifetime of being, save for his earliest years in Great Barrington, treated as a "nigger" in a country dominated by the capitalistic system, after observing how poorly that system served a great number of its constituency, he embraced what seemed to him its opposite, a system which, at least theoretically, favored increased participation by the very masses he saw excluded or exploited under capitalism. Accepting communism was not for him a way to avoid achieving justice for black Americans, but another way of attaining it more rapidly, along with attaining the same justice for all the people who did not possess it in the America he thought he knew.

His adoption of Ghanaian citizenship was his way of asserting his blackness at the time he was as a communist asserting his internationalism. He lived in Ghana, worked in Ghana, and seemed to know he would die in Ghana. He was entranced with the Ghana that could be, with the Ghana of Nkrumah's fascinating, compelling, and grand dreams. He was also grateful to aid the charismatic Nkrumah, and to receive Nkrumah's typically African reverence for the wisdom Du Bois as a very wise old man could bring to the new state.

When not ill he delighted in his Ghanaian life and made productive use of his time there, insisting that his role in creating the encyclopedia be recognized by his staff as real and not simply honorary. He enjoyed greeting selected visitors to his home on the calm green outskirts of Accra's swarming streets and enjoyed, too, occasional trips to outlying regions such as the lovely gardens at Aburi, where he walked under gigantic, vine-festooned trees, peaceful as Oedipus in the sacred groves. On 27 August 1963, Du Bois died in Ghana and was given a state funeral. In America, on 28 August, Roy Wilkins, the executive secretary of the NAACP—who had in 1934 succeeded Du Bois as editor of *Crisis*—reminded the quarter of a million Americans massed around the Lincoln Memorial for a civil rights demonstration, that Du Bois "was the voice calling to you to gather here today in this great cause."

The course of history seems in many ways inevitably impelled by innumerable converging forces barely if at all advanced, detained, or redirected by individual people or by the precise events they participate in. Perhaps the Zulu Empire would have been formed without Shaka, the South fought and conquered without Lincoln or Grant. Yet it is possible that some of the greatest movements in a nation's or our world's history, such as the constant search in America for a just government, can be influenced by individuals, their thoughts and actions, and by the impact they make upon other individuals and upon the masses. In this sense it is probable that William Edward Burghardt Du Bois made history in America and in Africa through his analyses of the race question, and through his quest for fair treatment of all people. Where we are now in America partly stems from where he tried to force and persuade us, mainly through education, to be. Along with his idols Frederick Douglass, John Brown, Sojourner Truth, and Harriet Tubman, along with Lincoln, Seward, and Sumner, along with those who came to prominence after him who, whether they acknowledged him or not, have been influenced by his perceptions of the racial and social situations in America, people like Malcolm X, Martin Luther King, Fannie Lou Hamer, and (strange compatriot!) Lyndon Johnson, he pushed America along the freedom road.

II *Darkness Visible:* The Black Flame

Although during his last years Du Bois's marriage to Shirley Graham brought him great personal satisfaction, and though the recognition he received on his world tours could have only

brightened his heart, Du Bois suffered much pain and intense
displeasure over many of the historic and personal events of the
late 1940s and 1950s. While, for example, the Supreme Court in
1954 outlawed segregation in the public schools, in 1956, Negroes
in Montgomery, Alabama, still had to boycott the city bus system
and confront local police so that they would be able to sit at the
front of the bus if they so desired. These were not good times,
politically, for black people, and in the midst of them, according
to Shirley Graham, Du Bois started his "Black Flame" trilogy.
Begun in 1952, *The Ordeal of Mansart* was published in 1957,
Mansart Builds a School in 1959, and *Worlds of Color* in 1961.
Leslie Lacy said of them that the trilogy "is neither a literary
success or as valuable as his scholarly works." Julius Lester
reported that "as novels" the books "fail completely. As fictionalized history, they are interesting, sometimes absorbing, and often
boring." Filled with racial horror stories and with a faltering
succession of blighted black lives, the "Black Flame" series, though
by any conventional measure an artistic flop, perhaps better than
any other single work by Du Bois communicates in its numbing
cumulative effect the violent antagonisms within Du Bois that he
attempted to suppress during the years he sought racial equity by
rational and scholarly means. The book further articulates the
deadly pessimism Du Bois so rarely permitted himself to express in
his quest for a just world.

Similar in technique to novels such as Upton Sinclair's Lanny
Budd series that attempts to blend fictional and historical events
and characters, the trilogy focuses on the career of the black
educator Manuel Mansart from his birth in 1876 to his death in his
seventy-eighth year. Definitely not a fictionalized double for Du
Bois (who appears disconcertingly in the series as "James
Burghardt"), Mansart is a representative Negro in Ralph Waldo
Emerson's sense of the term representative—an imperfect and yet
partially realized form of the ideal man who demonstrates how
high human aspirations can be achieved even while the person
achieving them displays human frailties. Mansart is baptized in
his lynched father's blood by his grandmother who calls him the
Black Flame: "I burn," he says when he is grown, "I almost
consume myself, I burn slow and dark but always, always. . . . I
burn for cleaning, not destroying. Therefore I burn slow." He
represents the black American seeking equality in a world dominated by racial and capitalistic oppression.

Manuel learns as a child to distrust whites and never totally rejects that learning, but as his education continues he also learns that many problems transcend race. In *The Ordeal of Mansart* he discovers that white farmers face "the same sort of oppression that Negroes faced. The same remedies applied to both." Far more naive and less cerebral and cynical than Du Bois, though shrewd and of superior intellect, Mansart climbs the long and slippery ladder of black success until he becomes president of the Georgia State Colored Agricultural and Mechanical College in Macon. Along the way he and his wife Susan (a negligible character) have four children. Mansart gradually sheds most of his illusions about the American way of life (although at one time he defends our war with Spain, he evolves into an adamant anti-imperialist), but never becomes as caustic and defiant as Du Bois—never really becomes what American journalists label a "black militant." On his deathbed in *Worlds of Color* he dreams first of London in ashes, Paris "a clot of blood," New York sinking into the ocean. But this image of a racial Armageddon is then replaced by heavenly visions of a presumably socialist future, where "China's millions lift . . . the soil of the nation" to build dams, and "the golden domes of Moscow shin[e] . . . on Russia's millions, yesterday unlettered, now reading the wisdom of the world."

Threaded through the books are passages narrating how Mansart's children develop in their increasingly separate lives. The first-born, Douglas, becomes a political boss in Chicago with Mafia-type connections. After a turbulent and unhappy marriage to a white woman, Revels, the next born, becomes a lawyer and finally a judge in New York City, and marries a highly intelligent and helpful black teacher. Revels early pursues his own gain in order to insulate himself from racial shocks, but ultimately he realizes his social responsibilities to fellow blacks. Bruce, the youngest son and most beloved by his mother, is handsome and athletic and big spirited, but he is eventually broken physically and psychologically by white assaults upon him, and while still a young man he commits suicide by confessing to a murder (in a distorted fashion echoing the death of Du Bois's own beloved son in childhood). Mansart's last child, Sojourner, is an ugly duckling until she finds personal satisfaction by playing the violin beautifully. Her husband, Roosevelt Wilson, helps her to attain an even greater sense of self-worth and dignity, and she successfully conspires with brother Douglas to buy him a bishopric in the African Methodist Episcopal church.

The novel's cast is augmented by Mansart's grandchildren and by families of whites whose lives intertwine with (often choking out) the lives of the black characters. Chief among these whites are the hypocritical old Southern plantation aristocrat Colonel Breckinridge, who is partly responsible for the death of Mansart's father; old John Pierce, a "typical, hard-bitten New England businessman" and bigot; John Baldwin, an educator who is at first just another racist but who comes to share many of Mansart's aspirations for black people (and who is viewed by his family and friends as a mad old man); and various Scruggs, a feral clan of murderous and corrupt poor whites not unlike Faulkner's Snopes family. As they intermarry, the whites become more sophisticated and smoother in their racism, and a few actually demonstrate sympathetic understanding of the black situation. One Scruggs (under his liberal wife's tutelage) becomes the Georgia secretary of labor, and in his own redneck way advances one of Du Bois's major themes in the trilogy, the need for harmony between black and white labor in the grip of a capitalistic oligarchy.

Rich in characters if not richly developed characters, the three books also focus upon many of the historical personages and events that filled the American and world scene from the 1870s to the 1950s, especially those relevant to black history. Sometimes these historical incursions illuminate the passing scene, sometimes they provide glimpses into Du Bois's perception of history, and sometimes one senses that Du Bois is settling an old score. The career of the Georgia legislator and sometimes populist Tom Watson is interestingly woven through several books, showing how political fortunes in the South are often formed upon and occasionally crushed under the race issue. Perhaps as a corrective to the conventional Southern white view of Henry Grady's supposedly enlightened concept of the New South, Du Bois portrays the entrepreneurial and journalistic genius as another example of a racist demagogue. A silly version of Teddy Roosevelt's notorious luncheon with Booker T. Washington is dramatized, bringing discredit to both men. Further material about Washington, sprinkled throughout all three books, seems sometimes necessary in a work so concerned with black history, sometimes gratuitous, and at least once (when Du Bois luridly narrates the events leading to Washington's death) decidedly venomous. The tragic life of Du Bois's occasional friend Monroe Trotter is more successfully integrated into the text, providing an excellent example of biography reinforcing theme. Surely Trotter was a gifted individual whose lifelong obsession with racial injustice eroded his spirit, making his suicide seem an almost logical act of the self-destruction racist America wanted from him. Watson, Washington, and Trotter are thus thematically connected, all demonstrating the corrosive force of bigotry. Grady's life shows how reputations can be made—and fortunes—by exploiting that bigotry.

Du Bois's use of real friends and foes is sometimes—as with Trotter—effective, and sometimes—as with Washington—not. Similarly, some of the information he supplies about himself ("no one in the student body liked his stiff, unsympathetic manners, his strict methods and impossibly high standards of work") is interesting; the trivia about Du Bois's second wife Shirley Graham is embarrassing; the comic-book depiction of Hitler and Stalin artistically foolish.

The primary historic deficiency of the three volumes is not that Du Bois imagined history where he should have stuck to reporting it, but that he imagined it so crudely and simplistically. Much of the data he supplies is informative and relevant, addressing the realities of black oppression. Statistics relating the numbers of black soldiers who fought in World War II for a democracy they never experienced at home, are very much to the political point he was aiming at. But this material is introduced without any skill, in authorial résumés or by characters who do not conduct dialogues but who exchange lectures. Moreover, when the forces that Du Bois attacks in the book are embodied in real or fictional people, they are too often ridiculous, one-dimensional, inconsistent, and erratic.

The student of Du Bois will find mainly familiar ideas in "The Black Flame" trilogy, but whether new or old these ideas are nowhere developed with the care and insight typical of him at his best. The accomplishments of black legislators during Reconstruction; the hypocrisy of white Christianity and the bluster and corruption of the black; the greed for colonies at the heart of both world wars; the domination of American education by business interests are all topics he essentially never changed his mind about. But too many of these ideas are discussed clumsily, as is the critique of his own "Talented Tenth" concept in *Worlds of Color*. Mansart comments after a stilted classroom dialogue that Du Bois "did not know the labor group in industry. If he had, he might have gone another path. As it was, his Talented [*sic*] became too often selfish money grabbers."

While Du Bois's career spanned that of novelists from Theodore
Dreiser to J. D. Salinger, from Charles Chesnutt to Ralph Ellison
and James Baldwin, he never learned much more about the
architectonics of fiction than he demonstrated in *The Quest of the
Silver Fleece*. That work had certain virtues as a historical
romance incorporating black history, but the Mansart trilogy fails
to match the panoramic sweep of the earlier book, perhaps
because its historic territory is far greater—practically boundless.
Similarly, while *The Quest of the Silver Fleece* gained in unity
through focusing around those elements of black history connected to the path cotton traveled from a seed to a wedding dress
fit for a black queen, the Mansart novels dissipate their energy
through wholesale inclusion of black history almost randomly
culled.

This failure to master significant form and to organize his
materials properly is highly unfortunate because, better than
anything else Du Bois wrote, with all its faults "The Black Flame"
communicates the mad violence of racism in America. In collaps-
ing the distinction between fact and illusion the books present a
world where the wildest, most paranoically induced nightmares of
conspiracy can turn out to be substantially true. The book is filled
with murders and suicides, some fictional, some historical, but all
contributing to a cumulative picture of the insane horror racial
prejudice lets run loose like a crazy fifth horseman through the
land. The lynchings and burnings Du Bois describes, or the scenes
where Mansart's son Douglas mows down white American officers
trapped between a group of black soldiers and the advancing
Germans, or where Mansart's youngest son Revels blows the head
off a vicious white policeman, must have emerged not only from
the collective history of black and white destruction but from the
private reservoir of fears and desires Du Bois had accumulated
over the years as a black man and race leader devoted to peace.

The novels also provide a few hints about some areas in Du
Bois's private life upon which he only occasionally touched in his
autobiographies. The books are filled with sexual maladjustments
most often between passionate males and reticent or seemingly
frigid women. Du Bois may be suggesting the general sexual
malaise of a sick modern world here, and he also may be reflecting
his own experience with his first wife. The novel otherwise repeats
a pattern observable in his other two novels, wherein the central
male protagonist joins with, and in important ways, submits to

the guidance of a strong and gifted woman—in the Mansart series the woman is Mansart's second wife Jean du Bignon—and the two form a union intellectually dominated by the woman. Clearly Du Bois's fiction shows that he desired a world where not only blacks and whites, but men and women were equals, where either might dominate through superior ability but not because of sexual privilege.

With so much of thematic and historic interest in the books it is unfortunate that they demonstrated a falling away from the ability Du Bois displayed in his first novel. His time scheme is especially erratic in the books, for he jumps back and forth through history and more than once errs in inaccurately aging his characters; for example, he makes mistakes in chronology with both Joe Scruggs the labor leader and Jean Du Bignon's grandmother. Sometimes the same information is repeated several times in the same book: worse, phrases like "soft cones of beauty" for "breasts" reveal Du Bois's old and sometimes destructive predilection for what he considered fine writing.

"Black Flame" is a badly flawed work, but one that despite its many failures portrays the terrifying ways that racial oppression in America can mutilate black life. The trilogy reveals also the faltering faith of its author in a better existence, in what he calls in *Worlds of Color* "the America that might be," a region removed from the agony and provincialism of race, "the world as one unified dwelling place."

III *Final Words: The* Autobiography

Recalling once more the days of his youth and years of his maturity in his *Autobiography* (1968), Du Bois returned to and even reprinted much of the matter contained in his earlier and less predominately personal racial biographies. The picture he gives of his childhood in the posthumously issued (in America) book perhaps deepens a few shadows or brightens up a highlight or two of the images he had previously presented, but he changes no outlines in any basic way nor adds any important new shapes. He remembers quite fondly and in detail his relationships to school chums and playmates, and recollects Great Barrington again as a kind of happy, golden valley of his green years. He tells of eating bread and drinking milk with his "slow-witted" buddy Farley Russell in the kitchen of the Russells' imposing home that was surrounded by a lovely flowered meadow dotted with fruit trees. Though the old man Du Bois declares at the outset of his *Autobiography* that "prejudiced I certainly am by my twisted life," the New England years he reports here do not seem to have exerted much negative influence on him. He emphasized the premium placed on success through hard work so dear to the New England way, and the pressures not to "give way to excessive emotion," but he views these regional demands as falling on black and white alike in New England.

The view he gives of his own family life is perhaps more somber than in the other books of memory. He sketches again with pride his family tree, but the glimpses he permits of his mother and father seem sadder than before. For the first time he calls his mother a "silent, repressed woman" who "sank into depression" after her husband left her. He mentions too the stroke she suffered late in her life which appears to have drawn young Du Bois even closer to her than many boys are to their mothers. Concerning his father, he is as reticent and relatively nonjudgmental as always, though he does mention that the town his father moved to, ostensibly to improve himself, was only forty miles south of Great Barrington, and suggests (the passage is typically ambiguous) that possibly he never or rarely wrote back to his wife after he departed forever.

Du Bois adds many details to the account of his own life after he too left Great Barrington, suggesting that he had more control over the course of his life than the earlier autobiographical reminiscences imply, underscoring, for example, that he chose to be withdrawn from his white classmates at Harvard, imposing upon himself a separation beyond that which Harvard forced him into. He is more open about his romantic and sex life as a young man, revealing that he was engaged to be married at Harvard, more significantly confessing to his own utter sexual innocence at Fisk and his early terror concerning physical relations with women. For the first time he admits that the wonderful years at Fisk were troubled by his sexual inexperience, for he was thrown into intimate contact with schoolmates whose sexual behavior and exploits could only have frightened him and made him feel inadequate. He also confesses that he lost his virginity when virtually raped by an affection-starved black woman, a mother to one of the students he taught in the back hills of Tennessee.

The book relates with justifiable bitterness Du Bois's shameful treatment during the 1950s by the Justice Department and his harassment by the federal government. His discussion of the trial and its aftermath shows that the experience did nothing to refreshen his faith in the "talented tenth" he once held so much hope for: "we must admit," he writes, "that the majority of the American Negro intelligentsia, together with much of the West Indian and West African leadership, shows symptoms of following in the footsteps of western acquisitive society." Saddest of all his memories of this time must have been his feeling that "the colored children [had] ceased to hear my name."

Du Bois's remarks about the acquisitiveness of many American, West Indian, and West African leaders underscore the more advanced Marxism he espoused during the period he was writing and compiling his *Autobiography.* "Part Two" of the book is in fact prefaced by a statement declaring himself a communist. "Part One" briefly narrates a triumphant tour he made of communist countries late in his life, after his federal trial. One familiar with Du Bois's life would probably read this chronologically misplaced segment of the book (prefacing as it does his birth) with mixed feelings of satisfaction and sadness. It was good that foreign countries honored Du Bois in ways his native land saw fit to avoid. In East Germany he received an honorary doctorate from his old Friederich Wilhelm (now renamed Humboldt) University. In China, another country honoring him, he said he "never felt the touch or breath of insult or even dislike—I who for 90 years in America scarcely ever saw a day without some expression of hate for 'niggers.' " It is sad, however, that Du Bois remained naive or blind in some of his perceptions of European politics. Irving Howe has charged that some of Du Bois's comments on contemporary politics read "as if they came from the very heart of a mimeograph machine," a contention no one would have made concerning his earlier polemics.[1] He writes about a Russia where "few police are in evidence, and there is little giving of orders. Secret dread? I sense none." More disturbing are his party-line platitudes about the Hungarian Revolt of 1965, caused he says by "pushing businessmen and artisans calling themselves 'Commons' and despising laborers and serfs, [who] rebelled against communism. . . . I was glad when the Soviet Union intervened and thus served notice on all reactionaries that the Russian Revolution was still unwilling to yield its gains before a show of force." The furious old warrior might be accused of too thoughtlessly embracing those who now embraced him not long after the time when his own

American nation had officially and unpleasantly intervened in his life, but it would be a mistake to consider his opinions those of a senile man.

Final assessment of the literary and ideological content of Du Bois's *Autobiography* is clouded by several details of its publication. According to its editor Herbert Aptheker, most of the manuscript was written in 1958–1959 and was subsequently "somewhat revised" by Du Bois in 1960. It was not published in America, however, until after his death, "as Dr. Du Bois wrote it," Aptheker says further in his preface to the book, with a few changes "of a technical nature" made apparently by the editor Aptheker. Presumably then Du Bois is responsible for the book's arrangement, although he never submitted the book for publication nor revised it as he always did, usually extensively, in proof. More troublesome, however, is the obvious fact that the book was not precisely written in 1958–1959 as much as it was assembled. Much of the writing in the *Autobiography* is either copied from Du Bois's earlier autobiographical works or is slightly revised from them. Peter Shaw, in his perceptive review of the book, says that its style is relatively "flat and matter of fact," but this is mainly true of the new material Du Bois composed and incorrect about the materials he lifted from his earlier books and apparently from letters and journals he kept. Chapter 6, for example, is a striking account of his childhood, but it is mainly a pastiche of *Darkwater* and *Dusk of Dawn*. Elsewhere, *The Souls of Black Folk* is employed, as are many of Du Bois's essays he never reprinted in book form. The result is a highly uneven text, which sometimes does not seem to be a finished book at all, but rather some passages from various sources that might be assembled into a book with rigorous reworking.

Granted the eclectic nature of the text, its ideological validity is not always easy to determine. Rayford Logan, Du Bois's co-worker and always astute concerning him, has pointed out a number of passages where significant revisions were made in original texts later incorporated into the published *Autobiography*.[2] For example, Du Bois wrote in a 1944 essay attacking the inadequacy of American communist strategy for blacks, that the communist program was "suicidal." In the later book the program is termed "inadequate for our plight." One would like to know when this correction was substituted and under what circumstances, before attempting to determine its importance to the history of Du Bois's evolving thought, for surely the attitudinal shift it demonstrates is significant. Perhaps final assessment of the literary and autobiographic value of Du Bois's last major work will have to await a study of its texts and their transformations.

Despite the murkiness surrounding some elements of the *Autobiography*, it is clear that Du Bois's autobiographical volumes, his racial biographies, are an integral part of a very old tradition in American life and literature extending back to William Bradford and his *Of Plimouth Plantation*. American men and women have constantly sought to define themselves by identifying the people to whom they belong, by examining the relationship between this people and the social and political landscape surrounding them. Shaw states in his review that the *Autobiography* is both public and private, personal and historical. Its reflexive light illuminates Du Bois's life and times and perhaps distorts both the man he was and the ages he lived in, as light from such a powerful source would create through the shadows and highlights it produced its own version of reality, but always shows brilliantly the impossibility of separating the man from his times. He was a man molded by the land, who helped to mold the land that shaped him. His *Autobiography* and his racial autobiographies reveal a human being who refused to be the failure his native country set him up to be, black, fatherless, "twisted" by racism, but nearly always looking forward to ways he could use his life to better the lives of his world.

CHAPTER 7

Summation

THE centennial of Du Bois's birth focused attention upon the man and his works, offering an opportunity for perhaps the first time in cool retrospect to crystallize public and professional opinion concerning the combative scholar and race leader who, during his argument-filled lifetime, seemed consciously to resist efforts to pin him down ideologically, or to characterize exactly his impact upon the American and Afro-American cultures that had produced him and that he had worked to change. The many nostalgic, parochial, hysterical, and critical reflections upon the kind of man he was and upon the concepts he held supposedly most consistently or most recently or predominately or ultimately, failed to produce a new, sharp, and clear representation of Du Bois, an image most could accept of who he was and what he stood for, such as we desire our men and women who are great writers or political leaders or educators to possess, so that we may facilitate their incorporation into our legends of history as heroes or villains. Du Bois's picture was not one that many would hang on their wall as a clear icon of some cherished ideal. Photographs of him spotlight his elitist's old-fashioned van Dyke goatee, his piercing blue eyes taking somebody's measure, his mouth almost never smiling but his lips set firmly, perhaps prior to voicing some cutting reply. His head is never sternly commanding like victorious, bald Lenin's; his arms are never spread to adoring masses like Martin Luther King's: his are nearly always bound in a suit with a tight vest. He would never be shown walking along a beach with his shoes off like sad, ruthless, wind-blown Bobby Kennedy.

The title of an astute article by Irving Howe suggests the problem that Du Bois presents to anyone seeking to encompass his significance as an American or world figure: "Remarkable Man, Ambiguous Legacy." Howe could have easily exchanged a few words in his title and written about an "Ambiguous Man and His Remarkable Legacy."[1] Though distance from the actual presence of the living Du Bois has brought dispassion to some who have observed him, it has also brought a kind of myopia, so that others have seen in him what they wanted to, or what they feared. The American Historical Association, whose members had generally avoided dealing during Du Bois's lifetime with his major works such as *Black Reconstruction*, devoted the first session of their 28 December 1968 meeting to "W. E. B. Du Bois (1868–1968); In Observance of the One-Hundredth Anniversary of His Birth." The same year, as Rayford Logan has reminded us, in Great Barrington citizens argued and "only after a bitter struggle" authorized "in 1969 a memorial park surrounding the site of the Du Bois family home."[2] Du Bois would have enjoyed the ironic commentary upon progress that these two events suggested, as he would have smiled with both appreciation and rue at Harvard's tardy recognition of him in their institute for the study of Afro-American studies that they named after him.

Perhaps the most obvious and yet strangest fact emerging from the backward glance over Du Bois's life that his centennial compelled is that looked at from the perspective of the myth of America propounded by countless glorifiers of the so-called American Dream, Du Bois exemplifies the American Success Story in its most popular form. Born poor, black, and fatherless in a village of sparse cultural attainments hardly worth more than a moment's notice, given a strong sense of self partly by his beloved mother's reliance upon and faith in him, urged toward seeing existence as a moral mission of high individual responsibility by both his mother and by the spiritual zeal of his region, identified by his neighbors as a promising youth possessing superior intelligence and aided considerably by them in his quest to obtain an exceptional education, helped by both their money and their emotional support, he worked hard at his studies, applied himself to goals involving both personal progress and the bettering of life for his fellow Americans, and ultimately became a recognized leader in his nation. If he did not achieve great wealth he lived his adult life in a fashion far above the level attained by his parents or his parent's parents in terms of cultural opportunities, travel, and in terms of the social circles of which he was a member. A historian of American achievement would have to seek far to find a more quintessential example of success in America, a better instance of a man who had been born low and risen high through self-help and the aid of private citizens, as high in America as it was possible for a person to aspire, when that person is black.

In his most popular book, *The Souls of Black Folk*, Du Bois wrote about what it meant to be always aware of yourself as black and as American, and to be always perceived in America as black. But while he always very proudly accepted his blackness, and even when he might have desired otherwise was identifiably American in many of his tastes and attitudes, he also was painfully sensitive to his own humanity. This tripleness of self-image partly explains why his life was filled with paradox: sometimes his needs as a person harmonized, sometimes they clashed. In his Pan-Africanism, for example, he embraced an element of his Negro heritage as only a Negro could, just as when he insisted upon Africa's right to its history of past greatness and to political independence in the present, he was viewing the continent from a black point of view. However, his insight into Africa's internal politics was always affected—some might say distorted—by his American liberal's angle of vision which sometimes blinded him to African realities and to view the Sub-Saharan land more idyllically than a critically perceptive African quite probably would. While he was honored as a brother by many African leaders, toward the end of his career some of the younger African Pan-Africanists resisted or even resented what they perceived as his condescending tendency to place too great an emphasis upon how the talented tenth of black Americans might aid or (in his own case) direct African social and political growth.

When he ceased to be an American citizen and made the last journey of his life, he traveled to Ghana and lived there, thus underscoring his African heritage. Nkrumah, however, was probably the most cosmopolitan Anglophone African leader of his day, and moreover had graduated from Lincoln University in Pennsylvania. Du Bois coupled his departure from America and arrival in Ghana with a statement swearing allegiance to communism, an ideology he interpreted as offering an international framework for justice, and aiming to link the laboring classes of all nations together in a harmonious and good society. For decades prior to this act of union he had himself insisted that "peoples of color," the races of brown and yellow and red and black, should recognize their common bonds of oppression and inequality. While much of his hostility was always directed toward Caucasians who dominated the world power structure although constituting a minority of its peoples, he clearly hoped for understanding between poor whites, the powerless of all races, and women who might unite to achieve the world that he longed for which would treat all fairly. Still, he was no saint and he hated as strongly as he loved. His hatred for aspects of the West coupled with his desire for a sensible world order, distorted by an intellectual arrogance that was an unlovely part of him also, could lead him astray from his just goal sometimes, for example, when he expressed a harshly Stalinist sympathy for the forces that crushed the Hungarian rebellion in 1965.

Physically a mixture of races, he was, perhaps despite himself, culturally mixed and eclectic in his tastes. But though he spoke with many voices he did not wear a mask. He knew the value of slave spirituals and African carvings, and of Beethoven and Brahms. He praised Eugene O'Neill and Langston Hughes, respected Alexander Crummel and Mary White Ovington, praised the black masses who tried to make Reconstruction work, and lauded congressmen Seward and Stevens whom he felt wanted to create a political environment where Negroes could freely participate in a democratic government. He knew that the source of his race's and his own life's blight was white racism, but he knew that no race possessed a monopoly upon corruption and venality, nor could the people of any race escape pain and grief and death: he realized also that racism unnecessarily increased black pain and brought about premature death to Negroes.

His greatest achievement as a writer was that he showed how extensive, how pervasive was the radical discrimination practiced on American soil from the time of the earliest settlements on it, how white Americans had profited from the work and exploitation of black Americans, how a system of legal and illegal oppression of black Americans was permitted to develop and was often sanctioned by the highest powers in the land, how the country grew fat on the sorrow and degradation it forced upon black Americans. *The Suppression of the African Slave-Trade to the United States of America, 1683–1870* demonstrated the moral failure of the new democracy to deal with its most undemocratic institution, partly because slavery was or seemed to be profitable, partly because of what appeared to be a politically expedient compromise which turned into a terrible political mistake costing hundreds of thousands of lives and national misery too great to

reckon. Adapted from his doctoral dissertation, the book combined a scholarly thoroughness and style with an as yet sheathed
but still operative moral zeal that would distinguish all of Du
Bois's best works.

The Philadelphia Negro documented a specific manifestation of
the nation's failure to grant Negroes the same social, economic,
and political choices it guaranteed most whites. As *The Suppres-*
sion of the Slave-Trade offered a longitudinal, historical review of
the unequal treatment afforded blacks kidnapped from African
homes and owned as physical property in the United States, *The*
Philadelphia Negro depicted in a lateral, sociological study the
condition of blacks in one American city, piling up masses of
statistics which collectively portrayed the nearly insurmountable
obstacles placed in the way of the Negroes, preventing them from,
except in rare individual instances, access to the bounties of
American life. Not content merely to compose graphs and grids
and tables of despair, Du Bois humanized the predicament of the
urban blacks he lived among by sketching and vividly dramatizing
the reality of their sometimes wretched, sometimes joyous existence, demanding that the humanity their surrounding society
wished to deny them be recognized and nourished.

In *The Souls of Black Folk* and to lesser degrees in *Darkwater,*
Dusk of Dawn, and his *Autobiography,* he formed from his own
experiences and his abilities as a historian, sociologist, and creative artist, a sensitive analysis of black life past and present so
powerful and compelling that for many black and white Americans he became a spokesman for the race, a representative Negro,
a mythic, archetypal figure. However, unlike most legendary
American success stories he was black and an intellectual and he
lived a long time, too long perhaps to remain popular, too often
corrosive in his criticisms to remain a spokesman for anyone but
himself. During the years when most of his best writing was done
and when he was most influential as a public figure, it is
impossible to extricate Du Bois the man from his work as a fighter
for Negro rights and from the literature he produced examining
aspects of blackness. As an official of the NAACP and editor of its
chief publication *Crisis,* author of one of the most personal black
narratives ever written and a scholar of undenied reputation, he
created an image of his race that so permeated the American and
black American cultures that it will be forever a part of them even
though the once shining light of his own name may have dimmed:

but recognized or not, he is firmly in the picture of black life that he created. He did not invent the Negro or the new Negro, but he wove himself into the design of blackness that, disliked or praised, forms so strong a motif in the patterns of twentieth-century American life. The reconstruction of his life as a private and public person, the many illustrations he offers from the lives of black men and women, the social and political and economic analyses he supplies are all mixed together in the four books which I have called racial biographies, or racial autobiographies, blending fact and feeling, passion and scholarship, real self and legend as he wished others to know him, and culminating in one varied, uneven, yet connected work, forming a powerful epic of black life.

Sometimes in delineating areas of the black experience Du Bois faltered, at least in terms of the firm strong strokes he employed in his major successes. The biography of John Brown is not always accurate and is source ridden, as are *The Negro* and *The Gift of Black Folk*, but each of these works made valuable contributions to the history of the race problem. *John Brown* emphasized the absolute rightness of its protagonist's attack upon slavery; in it Du Bois insisted that not Brown but contemporary American society was mad to permit chattel slavery to exist within its domain—and that the corrupt institution which allowed slavery in Brown's time was still present, as evidenced by the existence of disfranchised, undereducated, vocationally deprived, and poverty-ridden blacks. *The Negro* and *The Gift of Black Folk*, though thin in informational texture compared to Du Bois's first two great works, and sometimes aberrant in their judgments, were and are still rich fare for generations of Americans malnourished on white fantasies of Africa's uncivilized barbarism and often totally uninformed about the contribution of black America to the nation's culture and history.

Similarly his novels, at least the *Quest of the Silver Fleece* and the Mansart trilogy, presented some of the basic details of American Negro life even though not achieving the high merit of his best nonfictional work. These novels accurately portrayed many of the problems and joys of average and exceptional blacks trying to cope with an inimical environment containing both the common social and existential forces pressing down upon any underdog in contemporary society and the special pressures reserved for blacks in a white world. They presented positive images of strong, intelligent black men and women, and portrayed also the many black victims America's landscape is littered with, men and women "twisted" as Du Bois admitted even he was twisted, but destroyed also as he was not. His novels are admittedly more powerful in their evocation of the social, economic, and political context his characters live in than they are in the artistry of language, characterization, and structure critics rightly expect from major or even consistently good and popular novelists. Du Bois's novels, like his more successful poems such as "A Litany at Atlanta" and "The Burden of Black Women," were undertaken at least as much to compensate for the failure of American letters to deal with the gritty details of black life, as to enable Du Bois to express his creative and artistic imagination.

Black Reconstruction fuses Du Bois's scholarly and creative powers more effectively than any other single work, save possibly *The Souls of Black Folk*, which though it may illuminate blackness more brilliantly and intensely during its relatively brief duration, lacks *Black Reconstruction*'s great, sustained flood of light. While it is sometimes a bulky book, *Black Reconstruction* possesses the scholarly control of technique and subject evident in the less overwhelming *Suppression of the African Slave-Trade;* the general feel for humanity that helps save *The Phildelaphia Negro* from academic dessication; the moral zeal of *John Brown* without the moral blinders of that passionate but historically unsatisfying work. Richer in characterization than any of his novels and as filled with sharp polemic as the best journalism from *Crisis*, *Black Reconstruction* destroys old myths about the black past and its supposed history of incompetence and nonachievement and helps create, by showing the accomplishment of Negroes in the harrowing years after the Civil War, a sense of the possibilities of the black future, and of the American future: Du Bois was careful to note the many occasions before and during the Reconstruction period when some white Americans fought as John Brown had fought against the injustice Negroes faced in their struggle for equality.

Because of the unique situation of Negroes in American life, it is more difficult to assess Du Bois's actual political contributions and limitations as a race leader, than it is to evaluate his successes and failures as a writer. Had Du Bois been white, one could refer to the offices he held either elected or appointive, to specific pieces of legislation he might have authored or policies he put into effect, to firm accomplishments attributable to his power or influence or organizational skill. The highest offices he held were not political in the ordinary sense. That he was originator and general secretary of the fledgling Niagara Movement, director of publicity and research and member of the board of directors of the NAACP and editor of its magazine, *Crisis*, reflects the esteem with which he was held and suggests the authority he commanded within the black and civil rights communities in America. The central position he occupied for many years at successive Pan-African congresses attests to his international reputation as does the interest shown in him by Africa's leading politicians and thinkers. Further, even his unsuccessful 1950 New York senatorial campaign—which occurred during an unpropitious period in American politics for progressive candidates—suggests that even at this time in his career his name was still important and respected among the luckless followers of left-wing minority politics.

The testimony of wise and disparate Americans concerning the impact he made upon them and upon millions of other Americans is another gauge of his importance as a race leader. Though testimonials should be suspect in an age when the worst of people, books, films, and ideas in general can somehow secure blurbs and shills to witness the greatness of whatever shoddy person or product or chic trend is being hawked from cigarette to presidential hopeful, the quality of praise for Du Bois is notably high, especially considering that he operated during the last seven decades of his life very much in the public eye, often as an irritant. Though he could be warm and friendly to individuals he could also be obdurate and cold and harshly critical: some of his most basic ideas have come under heavy attack even by those who admired him, ideas such as what was perceived as his integrationism, his segregationism, his socialism and communism and elitism, his anti-Americanism. Many of course attacked him because he was proudly black, others such as Marcus Garvey because he seemed to be too white (and it is true that his cultural preferences always included elements he assimilated from white Western society). Some were antipathetic to his style of operation because it lacked the warm vitality and intimacy often associated with black street or farm life—because Du Bois was an "intellectual." Others, including not a few black academicians, questioned the depth of his scholarly commitment. Yet Du Bois is perhaps the one omnipresent black leader of the twentieth century, a single

focal point of terrific intellectual energy who made a recognized
contribution—accepted or attacked—to nearly every area of
black life in America.

Ample testimony to Du Bois's importance as a public figure—
often from individuals who were or would have been extremely
uncomfortable with him as a person or as a thinker—demonstrates
the major role he played in black American (and by logical
extension American) life. At one time Du Bois was simply an
assumed part of black awareness. As the playwright Lorraine
Hansberry, wrote "I do not remember when I first heard the name
Du Bois. For some Negroes it comes into consciousness so early, so
persistently, that it is like the spirituals or the blues or discussions
of oppression." The historian John Henrik Clarke called him "truly
the father of the modern Black liberation movement, the twentieth-century leader of the struggle against racial oppression and
discrimination."[3]

Yet perhaps his most perceptive, thorough, and objective critic,
Francis Broderick, while stating that Du Bois had "for thirty years
. . . made himself the loudest voice in demanding equal rights for
the Negro and in turning Negro opinion away from the acceptance
of anything less," titled one of his discussions of Du Bois, "A
Leader Without Followers." Whatever the validity of Broderick's
appellation, we can assess Du Bois's significance as a writer and as
a race leader by suggesting that no one who came after him was
precisely like him, combined his talents, mixed his amazing
abilities with the degree of success that he attained—no one who
was black and no one who was white. Poet, novelist, essayist,
journalist, editor, polemicist, propagandizer, scholar, teacher,
activist, another paradox of W. E. B. Du Bois is that the very
breadth of his accomplishments perhaps makes impossible the
ordinary ways to measure the component elements of his importance. The magnitude of his interests and achievements, the
complexity of his character, somehow distances him from his
audience as Martin Luther King and Malcolm X are not—as
Thomas Jefferson is distant from us as a hero and George
Washington is not. Perhaps this, along with his prickliness and
penchant for controversy, explains why today he seems not as
central a figure as he should be. Shoved from the white consciousness as the contentious Malcolm X was shoved since his assassina-
tion, Du Bois does not appear to exercise the same hold upon the

black community that he once commanded: clearly he will always be a hard man to grasp and retain.[4]

An agitator who made his country and even his fellow black Americans often feel uncomfortable, Du Bois was a man for all seasons but never a man for all fashions and indeed never really a fashionable man in the world of ideas. To remove the overlapping of his images to resolve the paradox of his life would be to unravel his essential self which was at heart comprised of a bundle of strangely harmonious contradictions. How could he have otherwise endured his twoness as a black and as an American, as a lover and attacker of the life around him: how could he have survived without coming apart, had he not bound together tightly the lines of his life? It might be instructive, however, to contemplate for a moment how he might have lived otherwise, how productively he might with all his skills have channeled his activities into some one employment, some one way to achieve a dream, had he been able to live differently; not white in America, for to have lived white would have changed his nature completely and turned him away from so much that identified and sustained him, but had he been born, say, black in an America not necessarily free from racism but at least as aware of his legitimate human needs and as responsive to his special genius as his fellow townspeople were in Great Barrington when he was a boy. But this sea change would involve all its contemplaters in magical thinking, for a shift in his existence would assume a like shift in his country's treatment of other unexceptional and exceptional blacks, would demand a transformation in attitudes toward all the second-rated in America and the world who, as Du Bois perceived their fate, were not treated fairly.

Yet the reality of his success as a writer and race leader is more important as fact than fantasy precisely because, surprisingly enough, born poor and black he spoke out for change and transformation and was heard over the changing world: black, American, Ghanaian, he carved his initials in the universe.

Notes and References

Chapter One

1. When writing about his life, Du Bois (pronounced Du Boyce) often repeated himself from book to book. The phrase "the golden river," for example, occurs in biographic sections of *Darkwater, Dusk of Dawn*, and the *Autobiography*. In this chapter on Du Bois's life, and generally elsewhere, I use the text of the *Autobiography* for quotations, except where I indicate otherwise.

I have tried to eliminate footnotes whenever possible without confusing the reader. I have not ordinarily cited page references to Du Bois's books, though in my text I have tried to make clear where passages may be located, for example, by supplying the chapter heading of a citation. All letters quoted, unless I indicate otherwise, are from Aptheker's excellent edition of the *Correspondence*, which is fully indexed and arranged chronologically.

2. Herbert Aptheker, introduction to *The Correspondence of W. E. B. Du Bois*, vol. 1, *1877-1934* (Amherst, 1973), p. xxv.

3. Shirley Graham (Du Bois), *His Day is Marching On, A Memoir of W. E. B. Du Bois* (Philadelphia, 1971), pp. 100, 108.

4. *Correspondence*, vol. 2, *1934-1944*, p. 168.

5. *Autobiography* (New York, 1968), p. 121. Interestingly enough, Du Bois did not include this unpleasant anecdote in *Dusk of Dawn*, though he has a section in the book devoted to how his "knowledge of the race problem became more definite" during his years at Fisk.

6. There is now a W. E. B. Du Bois Institute for Afro-American Research at Harvard.

7. Francis L. Broderick, *W. E. B. Du Bois, Negro Leader in a Time of Crisis* (Stanford, 1959), p. 21, has interesting comments on this point.

8. Correspondence, 1: 28.

Chapter Two

1. Broderick, p. 31.

2. In the *Correspondence*, 1: 40, he says he was paid $900.

3. *Autobiography*, p. 197.

4. The quotation from James is from his *The Will to Believe*, and its implications are discussed in Richard Hofstadter's *Social Darwinism in American Thought* (Boston, 1955), p. 130 and passim.

5. Myrdal mentions Du Bois's book on p. 1132 of his magisterial study. The appraisals of Du Bois by Frazier, Drake, Cayton, and others are in Elliot Rudwick's highly illuminating essay, "W. E. B. Du Bois as a Sociologist," in *Black Sociologists: Historical and Contemporary Perspectives*,ed. Blackwell and Janowitz (Chicago, 1974), pp. 25—55.

Chapter Three

1. In W. E. B. Du Bois, *A Profile*, ed. Rayford W. Logan (New York, 1971), p. 224. But Du Bois probably studied theories of race in Germany during his student years there around 1892, and this would have necessitated some study of Africa.

2. *Pan-Africanism, A Short Political Guide* (New York, 1965), p. 24.

3. Legum, p. 25.

4. (London, 1973), p. 89.

5. Quoted in Legum, p. 29.

6. "The Negro Church," in *The Seventh Son, The Thought and Writings of W. E. B. Du Bois*, ed. Julius Lester (New York, 1971), p. 251.

7. *W. E. B. Du Bois, A Reader*, ed. Meyer Weinberg (New York, 1972), p. 379.

8. See William Leo Hansberry's account of the effect Du Bois had upon his African research and that of others, in "Du Bois' Influence on African History," *Freedomways* 5 (Winter 1965): 73–87.

9. See especially August Meier's "The Paradox of W. E. B. Du Bois," in *W. E. B. Du Bois, A Profile*, ed. Rayford Logan, p. 72.

10. Redding mentions the responses of Johnson and Abrahams in his introduction to *The Souls of Black Folk* (New York, 1961), p. ix. Comments by Weber and James are in the Correspondence, 1: 106 and 134 respectively. James's response was included in his book *The American Scene*.

11. Ferris's very interesting contemporary estimation of Du Bois was originally published in 1913 and can be found in Logan's *W. E. B. Du Bois, A Profile*, pp. 86–121. Logan has edited Ferris's text somewhat and titles it "The Emerging Leader—A Contemporary View." The quotation I have used from Ferris is on p. 87.

12. *Correspondence*, 1: 153, and "The Historian," in *W. E. B. Du Bois, A Profile*, p. 262.

13. Many of the historical weaknesses of the book, together with Du Bois's reaction to the adverse criticism it received, are mentioned in the exchange of letters between Paul Elmer More (then editor of the *Nation*),

Du Bois, and Du Bois's soon-to-be-colleague at the NAACP, Oswald Garrison Villard, in *Correspondence*, 1: 153–59.

14. This is the conclusion to the earliest editions of the text. For a new edition published in 1962, Du Bois kept the last three paragraphs of the early text but inserted before them several pages of Stalinist declarations.

Chapter Four

1. *Correspondence*, 1: 223.

2. *The Seventh Son*, p. 73. Christopher Lasch discusses in *The New Radicalism in America* the reasons why a number of liberals and left-leaning ideologues of the day changed their attitude toward the war by eventually supporting America's role in it. Often a maverick, Du Bois was also a traditional liberal in many ways, and should not be viewed as totally separate from the liberal tradition.

3. *The Crisis*, September 1933, quoted in Henry Lee Moon, *The Emerging Thought of W. E. B. Du Bois* (New York, 1972), pp. 66, 64. Du Bois did not, however, interpret the phrase "black skin" literally, as Garvey sometimes did, although during one of his disagreements with Walter White he claimed that White did not have the same problems in white society that darker skinned Negroes had.

4. *Correspondence*, 1: 113.

5. That Du Bois saw conditions in the cotton industry accurately can be validated by comparing his novel to such standard analyses as David L. Cohn's *The Life and Times of King Cotton* (New York, 1956), and Rupert B. Vance's *All These People* (Chapel Hill, 1948).

6. This theme is addressed in Jack B. Moore, "Frank Yerby: The Guilt of the Victim," *Journal of Popular Culture* 8 (Spring 1975): 746-56.

7. *Correspondence*, 1: 177.

8. To name but two important works he could have made use of but did not, he neglected to read Lord Lugard's *Political Memoranda* (London, 1906) or D. D. Morel's *Nigeria, Its People and Problems* (London, 1912).

9. An excellent historical narrative describing the pogrom is Charles Crowe's "Racial Massacre in Atlanta, September 22, 1906," *Journal of Negro History*, 54 (April 1969): 150-73.

10. The story foreshadows materials later science fiction writers would employ, such as Richard Matheson in *I Am Legend* (filmed several times, most recently as *The Omega Man*).

11. Arnold Rampersad, *The Art and Imagination of W. E. B. Du Bois* (Cambridge, 1976), p. 184. See also Darwin Turner's "W. E. B. Du Bois and the Theory of a Black Aesthetic," *Studies in the Literary Imagination* (Atlanta, 1975), pp. 1-21, for a persuasive discussion of Du Bois's important role in establishing a black aesthetic.

12. Ibid., p. 198.

13. For the rejoinder to Mencken, see Weinberg, *W. E. B. Du Bois*, *A Reader*, p. 262. For the failure of the Renaissance, *ibid.* p. 181.

14. Du Bois's speech is mentioned in Christopher Lasch's *The Agony of the American Left* (New York, 1969), p. 48.

15. "Pan-Africanism as Romantic Racism," in *W. E. B. Du Bois*, *A Profile*, p. 236. In Amritjit Singh's *The Novels of the Harlem Renaissance: Twelve Black Writers, 1923-1933* (University Park, Penn., 1976), Singh contends that "with the exception of [Claude McKay's] *Banjo*, *Dark Princess* is the only novel from the Harlem Renaissance that exhibits a full awareness of the African and Asian non-white masses." Arnold Rampersad in "W. E. B. Du Bois As a Man of Literature," *American Literature* 51 (March, 1979) notes that the book is the first novel "to identify and promulgate the doctrine of the third world." But the doctrinal awareness seems almost ludicrous in the context of the book. Herbert Aptheker's introduction to his reprint of the novel (New York, 1974) mentions some of the real people and events the novel is based upon.

Chapter Five

1. "The Historian," in *W. E. B. Du Bois*, *A Profile*, p. 251.

2. *Correspondence*, 2:19.

3. "An Analysis of Some Reconstruction Attitudes," *Journal of Southern History* 12 (November, 1946): 475. Unfortunately, not all historians advanced as close to the "truth" as Du Bois. Early during his planning of civil rights policy, President Kennedy operated from the older view of the Reconstruction, exemplified in his depiction of Thaddeus Stevens in *Profiles in Courage* as a crippled, fanatic radical. Arthur Schlesinger commented in *Robert Kennedy and His Times* (New York, 1978), p. 350, "Alas, thus he had been taught by the Harvard history department." The murder of Medgar Evers changed Kennedy's mind. Faulty history is dangerous.

4. The Scottsboro case was similar to the Sacco-Vanzetti case and the Rosenberg case in generating fierce partisan enthusiasms, generally pitting liberals and radicals against the prosecuting state authority. Nine Negro men were accused of raping two white women in a box car in Alabama. The trial was held in Scottsboro, Alabama, and the original verdict condemned eight of the young men to death (the case of the ninth resulted in a mistrial). At the time of the trial, local prejudices were such that a fair verdict was impossible. The case was appealed and eventually four defendants were given reduced sentences, while rape charges against the others were dropped.

Chapter Six

1. "Remarkable Man, Ambiguous Legacy," *Harper's* 236 (March 1968): 143.
2. In *W. E. B. Du Bois, A Profile*, p.xiv.

Chapter Seven

1. *Harper's*, pp. 143-149.
2. *W. E. B. Du Bois, A Profile*, pp. vii, viii.
3. The tributes of Clarke and Hansberry, together with other words and articles in praise of Du Bois may be found in the special Du Bois issue of *Freedomways* 5 (Winter, 1965).
4. It is difficult to ascertain the extent of a historical figure's hold upon the popular imagination. My casual observation of the homes of black people in West Africa and in America has revealed many iconographic pictures of the Kennedys, Martin Luther King, Jr., Frederick Douglass, Malcolm X, Bobby Seale, Angela Davis, and others, but I have almost never seen a picture of W. E. B. Du Bois, though doubtless such pictures exist. A promotional, public service advertisement sponsored by a commercial enterprise which appeared in many black-oriented magazines in the winter of 1978, depicting a gallery of famous black Americans, did not include Du Bois's picture. I can only conclude from such hints that Du Bois's stature as a folk hero is declining.

Selected Bibliography

PRIMARY SOURCES

Du Bois was an exceptionally prolific writer who published work of some kind from his adolescence until his death. Paul G. Partington's *W. E. B. Du Bois: A Bibliography of His Published Writings* is "the most complete bibliography of Du Bois's writings ever published." Aptheker's *Annotated Bibliography* is extensive, and even a selected bibliography such as Meyer Weinberg's in *W. E. B. Du Bois, A Reader,* lists over sixty items in his "Books, Pamphlets, and Addresses" section, over sixty "Chapters in Books," and fifteen items of "Fiction and Poetry." Ernest Kaiser's "Selected Bibliography" in *Freedomways* is similarly lengthy. Helpful bibliographies are also contained in Francis Broderick's *W. E. B. Du Bois: Negro Leader in a Time of Crisis;* Elliot Rudwick's *W. E. B. Du Bois, A Study in Minority Leadership;* Leslie Lacy's *Cheer the Lonesome Traveler;* and Rayford W. Logan's *W. E. B. Du Bois, A Profile.* The latter two include brief comments on selected works. In general, I have listed only what I consider Du Bois's major books.

Suppression of the African Slave-Trade to the United States of America. New York: Longmans, Green, 1896.

Morality Among Negroes in Cities. Edited by Du Bois. Atlanta Study no. 1. Atlanta: Atlanta University Press, 1896. Du Bois edited fourteen of these studies from 1896 to 1909, and co-edited with A. G. Dill, four more from 1910 to 1914. Many are reprinted in the Atlanta University Publications (New York: Arno Press and the *New York Times,* 1968).

The Philadelphia Negro. Philadelphia: Publishers for the University, 1899.

The Souls of Black Folk. Chicago: A. C. McClurg, 1903.

John Brown. Philadelphia: G. W. Jacobs, 1909.

The Quest of the Silver Fleece. Chicago: A. C. McClurg, 1911.

The Negro. New York: Henry Holt, 1915.

Darkwater: Voices from Within the Veil. New York: Harcourt, Brace & Howe, 1920.

The Gift of Black Folk. Boston: Stratford, 1924.

Dark Princess: A Romance. New York: Harcourt, Brace, 1928.

Africa, Its Geography, People and Products. Girard, Kansas: Haldeman-Julius, 1930.

Africa, Its Place in Modern History. Girard, Kansas: Haldeman-Julius, 1930.

Black Reconstruction in America, 1860–1880. New York: Harcourt, Brace, 1935.

The Revelation of Saint Orgne, the Damned. Nashville: Hemphill, 1939.

Black Folk, Then and Now. New York, Henry Holt, 1939.

Dusk of Dawn: An Essay Toward an Autobiography of a Race Concept. New York: Harcourt, Brace, 1940.

Color and Democracy. New York: Harcourt, Brace, 1940.

The World and Africa. New York: Viking Press, 1947. 2d ed. New York: International Publishers, 1965.

In Battle for Peace: The Story of My 83rd Birthday. New York: Masses and Mainstream, 1951

The Ordeal of Mansart. New York: Mainstream Publishers, 1957. This and the next two titles form the *"Black Flame"* trilogy.

Mansart Builds a School. New York: Mainstream Publishers, 1959.

Worlds of Color. New York: Mainstream Publishers, 1961.

The Autobiography of W. E. B. Du Bois: A Soliloquy on Viewing My Life from the Last Decade of its First Century. New York: International Publishers, 1968.

Herbert Aptheker has overseen the reprinting of a number of Du Bois's books in recent years, and written introductions to them. More are forthcoming, published by the Kraus-Thomson Organization Limited, Millwood, New York.

SECONDARY SOURCES

Only items of especial significance to the present study are listed. I have also noted here several particularly helpful collections or reprintings of Du Bois's work in which various editors have made substantial critical or biographic contributions. Herbert Aptheker's introductions to works in the Kraus-Thomson reprint series should be consulted when available.

APTHEKER, HERBERT. *Annotated Bibliography of the Published Writings of W. E. B. Du Bois.* Millwood, N.Y: Kraus-Thomson Organization, 1973. Extensive listing of books, magazine and newspaper articles, pamphlets, etc., with authoritative comments.

———. *The Correspondence of W. E. B. Du Bois.* Amherst: University of Massachusetts Press, 1973-1978. Volume 1 (1877-1934), volume 2 (1934-1944), volume 3 (1944-1963). An indispensable collection with exceptionally helpful and interesting notes by the eminent Marxist historian and friend of Du Bois, revealing the great range of Du Bois's interests and the care he took to correspond with ordinary people.

————. "The Historian," *Negro History Bulletin* 30 (April 1969): 6-16. Reprinted in Rayford S. Logan's *W. E. B. Du Bois, A Profile*, this essay briefly examines Du Bois's skills and limitations as a historian.

BRODERICK, FRANCIS L. "W. E. B. Du Bois: History of an Intellectual." In *Black Sociologists: Historical and Contemporary Perspectives*, ed. James E. Blackwell and Morris Janowitz. Chicago: University of Chicago Press, 1974. P. 3-24. A valuable review of Du Bois's intellectual career, emphasizing that he "provided the first reliable information about Negroes in America based on empirical sociological research."

————. *W. E. B. Du Bois, Negro Leader in a Time of Crisis*. Stanford: University Press, 1959. Although Du Bois lived some important years beyond the publication date of this book, it is still absolutely essential to an understanding of his life, his works, and the evolution of his thought. Scholarly, sensible, relatively sympathetic, and authoritative.

BRODWIN, STANLEY. "The Veil Transcended: Form and Meaning in W. E. B. Du Bois' *The Souls of Black Folk*." *Journal of Black Studies* 2 (March 1972): 303–21. A study of literary techniques in Du Bois's classic, focusing upon its "neo-Hegelian dialectic."

CONTEE, CLARENCE. "The Emergence of Du Bois as an African Nationalist." *Journal of Negro History* 54 (January 1969): 48–63. Clear and succinct review of Du Bois's role in the evolution of Pan-Africanism.

DIGGS, IRENE. "Du Bois and Women: A Short Story of Black Women, 1910-1934." *Current Bibliography on African Affairs* 7 (Summer 1974): 260–307. In this deceptively titled, thoroughly documented article, Du Bois's former research assistant discusses at length his constant concern for the predicament of black women.

DU BOIS, SHIRLEY GRAHAM. *His Day is Marching On*. Philadelphia: J. B. Lippincott, 1971. Du Bois's second wife, herself a writer, succeeds in portraying Du Bois as a real and humane man in her shrewd and touching memoir of him, making her work unique among Du Bois biographies.

ELDER, ARLENE. "Swamp Versus Plantation: Symbolic Structure in W. E. B. Du Bois' *The Quest of the Silver Fleece*." *Phylon* 34 (December 1973): 358–67. Concludes that the swamp represents "all that is free, wild, joyful, and lovely" while the plantation is "all that is exploitative." Notes also that Du Bois "avoids . . . simplistically equating the swamp with black life and the plantation with white."

FONER, PHILLIP S. *W. E. B. Du Bois Speaks: Speeches and Addresses.* 2 vols. New York: Pathfinder Press, 1970. Although Du Bois was not known as one who mesmerized large crowds to action this judicious collection reveals his high skills and wide range as a speaker who could appeal to various kinds of audiences.

FERRIS, WILLIAM H. "The Emerging Leader—A Contemporary View," In Rayford W. Logan, *W. E. B. Du Bois, A Profile*, pp. 86–121. Originally written in 1913, this article presents a fascinating appraisal of Du Bois before he had acquired the stature and notoriety of his later years.

Freedomways 5 (Winter 1965). A W. E. B. Du Bois memorial issue devoted entirely to letters and articles praising and analyzing Du Bois and his work. Words of praise from Kwame Nkrumah, Nnamdi Azikiwe, Roy Wilkins, Paul Robeson, John Hope Franklin, and Langston Hughes are included along with scholarly essays treating Du Bois as a philosopher, historian, prophet, inspirational figure, etc. A book version of the issue edited by John Henrik Clarke and others was published as *Black Titan* (Boston: Beacon Press, 1970).

GREEN, DAN S. "Bibliography of Writings About W. E. B. Du Bois," *College Language Association Journal* 20 (March 1977): 410–21. This compilation contains books, articles, and dissertations about Du Bois, including a number of helpful studies by the bibliographer himself.

HANSBERRY, LEO. "Du Bois' Influence on African History." *Freedomways* 5 (Winter 1965): 73–87. A distinguished teacher of African history praises Du Bois for introducing many black scholars (including himself) and citizens to African history.

HARDING, VINCENT. "A Black Messianic Visionary," *Freedomways* 9 (1st quarter 1969): 44–58. Also reprinted in Rayford W. Logan's *W. E. B. Du Bois, A Profile*, pp. 274–93. A controversial, interesting argument emphasizing Du Bois's black nationalist tendencies. Logan disputes Harding's thesis.

HARLAN, LOUIS R. *Booker T. Washington: The Making of a Black Leader.* London: Oxford University Press, 1972. It is to be hoped that Du Bois will one day be the subject of a biography as authoritative as this one, which is absolutely necessary to an understanding of the Du Bois-Washington conflict.

HILL, MOZELL C. "The Formative Years of Phylon Magazine," *Freedomways* 5 (Winter 1965): 129–42. A brief history of Du Bois's early work with the distinguished magazine of race relations that he founded.

HOWE, IRVING. "Remarkable Man, Ambiguous Legacy," *Harpers* 236 (March 1968): 143–49. Offers a good resume of Du Bois's life and his contributions to American thought, but is puzzled by Du Bois's seeming blindness to the excesses of Stalin's regime, since they represented the kind of oppression Du Bois had always opposed. Howe also recollected that Richard Nixon thought the American Communist party was attempting to confuse right-minded Americans by employing the name "Du Bois Clubs" which sounded like "The Boys Clubs" (of America).

IJERE, MARTIN O. "W. E. B. Du Bois and Marcus Garvey as Pan-Africanists: A Study in Contrast," *Presence Africaine* 79 (1st quarterly 1974): 188–206. Concludes that while the two shared "a common faith in the destiny of Africa and people of African descent," they were "miles apart in their programmes."

INGERSOLL, WILLIAM T. Tape-recorded interview with W. E. B. Du Bois. As part of the Columbia University Historical Collection, this interview was recorded in 1960, and presents Du Bois reminiscing about his early years. The tape has been transcribed and is available on microfilm. Du Bois's memories are as always interesting, even when they disagree with some of his memories recollected elsewhere.

KAISER, ERNEST. "Selected Bibliography of the Published Writings of W. E. B. Du Bois." IN *Black Titan*, ed. John Henrik Clarke et al. New York, 1970. Pp. 309-30. An earlier version of this valuable bibliography was published in *Freedomways* 5 (Winter 1965): 207-13.

KELLOGG, CHARLES FLINT. *NAACP: A History of the National Association for the Advancement of Colored People*. Vol. 1. Baltimore: Johns Hopkins Press, 1967. A standard reference with substantial and objective treatment of Du Bois's relationship with the organization and its official publication *The Crisis*.

LACY, LESLIE ALEXANDER. *Cheer the Lonesome Traveler: The Life of W. E. B. Du Bois*. New York: Dell Publishing, 1970. Published in a series "particularly suitable for young adult readers," this sensitive and understanding report offers a clear picture of Du Bois's life and attainments for an adult audience as well. Especially good at explaining Du Bois's significance to young black Americans.

LANGLEY, J. AYODELE. *Pan-Africanism and Nationalism in West Africa, 1900-1945: A Study in Ideology and Social Classes*. London: Oxford University Press, 1973. Places Du Bois in the international context of leaders working for African unity, and pays special care to West African contributions to that goal.

LESTER, JULIUS. *The Seventh Son: The Thought and Writings of W. E. B. Du Bois*. New York: Random House, 1971. Offers well chosen excerpts from Du Bois's books and from his periodical articles, including some of his very early (1883) newspaper work. Lester's introduction is a book in itself, giving a spirited, penetrating, and sometimes opinionated overview of Du Bois and his works.

LOGAN, RAYFORD W., ED. *W. E. B. Du Bois, A Profile*. New York: Hill and Wang, 1971. An excellent collection of essays by Broderick, Meier,

Rudwick, Isaacs, and others, treating a range of Du Bois's interests, together with Logan's unusually acute, sensible, and unworshipful comments about his former colleague, a "complex personality" Logan says he "doubt[s] that anyone really knew."

MATHEWS, BASIL. *Booker T. Washington: A Biography.* Cambridge: Harvard University Press, 1948. See especially pp. 273–303, reprinted in Logan, *W.E.B. Du Bois, A Profile*, pp. 183–209 and titled "The Continuing Debate" for a good analysis of key issues in the Du Bois-Washington disagreement.

MEIER, AUGUST. *Negro Thought in America, 1880–1915: Racial Ideologies in the Age of Booker T. Washington.* Ann Arbor: University of Michigan Press, 1963. Excellent for the context of Du Bois's early civil rights operations. Logan, *W. E. B. Du Bois, A Profile*, reprints a section called "The Paradox of W. E. B. Du Bois," pp. 64–85, that is important to an understanding of Du Bois's character.

MOON, HENRY LEE. *The Emerging Thought of W. E. B. Du Bois.* New York: Simon and Schuster, 1972. "Essays and Editorials from *The Crisis* with an Introduction, Commentaries, and a Personal Memoir" by a former *Crisis* editor. The materials are well selected, and arranged by topics, for example, "Segregation" and "Of the Negro and the Arts."

MOSES, WILSON J. "The Poetics of Ethiopianism: W. E. B. Du Bois and Literary Black Nationalism," *American Literature* 47 (November 1975): 411-27. An informed discussion of Du Bois's relation to black nationalism in light of his particular fusion of Ethiopianism, "a literary-religious tradition common to English speaking Africans," with "the European tradition of interpretive mythology transplanted to America by its European colonizers."

NELSON, TRUMAN. Introduction to *The Gift of Black Folk.* New York: Washington Square Press, 1970. Pp. vii—xx. A brief, sensitive introduction to this work by a long-time student of Du Bois.

PARTINGTON, PAUL G. *W. E. B. Du Bois: A Bibliography of His Published Writings.* Whittier, California: printed by Penn Lithographers for Paul Partington, 1979 (revised edition). Begun in 1959, this bibliography is the most complete, a labor of scholarship that notes, among standard entries, reprints of Du Bois's books in foreign languages.

RAMPERSAD, ARNOLD. *The Art and Imagination of W. E. B. Du Bois.* Cambridge: Harvard University Press, 1976. Excellent extended discussions of key works and ideas, especially good on the backgrounds to and formation of Du Bois's thinking. Solid and scholarly.

———. "W. E. B. Du Bois As a Man of Literature." *American Literature* 51 (March 1979): 50–69. Concise and skillful analysis of Du Bois's literary achievements, contending that he was "the first black poet publicly to break with rhyme and blank verse," and the first "to identify and promulgate the doctrine of the third world" (in "A Litany at Atlanta" and *Dark Princess*).

Ross, B. Joyce. *J. E. Spingarn and the Rise of the NAACP, 1911–39.* New York: Atheneum, 1972. Contains many interesting insights on Du Bois's cherished friendship with the literary critic and civil libertarian, together with information on Du Bois's central and abrasive role in the NAACP.

Rudwick, Elliott M. "W. E. B. Du Bois as Sociologist." In *Black Sociologists*, ed. Blackwell and Janowitz, pp. 25-55. Identifies Du Bois as a pioneer sociologist "in the main ignored by the elite in the profession," and relates his methodology favorably to the more costly and complicated institutionally based methods used in the profession today.

————. *W. E. B. Du Bois, A Study in Minority Group Leadership.* Philadelphia: University of Pennsylvania Press, 1960. Reissued as *W. E. B. Du Bois, Propagandist of the Negro Protest* in 1968, this standard work investigates the chief events and controversies in Du Bois's career with sound scholarship, clarity, and sympathy.

Shaw, Peter. "The Uses of Autobiography." *American Scholar* 38 (Winter 1968-69): 136-50. Perceptive analysis of Du Bois's summing up, comparing it to Bertrand Russell's, which was published at the same time.

Shepperson, George. Introduction to *The Negro*, New York: Oxford University Press, 1970. Pp. vii-xxv. Contains a sensible critique of Du Bois's Africanism and his use of African source materials.

Singh, Amritjit. *The Novels of the Harlem Renaissance: Twelve Black Writers, 1923-1933.* University Park: Pennsylvania State University Press, 1976. Examines the philosophical and ethnic implications of *Dark Princess* while ignoring its aesthetic dreariness.

Stone, William B. "Ideolect and Ideology: Some Stylistic Aspects of Norris, James, and Du Bois." *Style* 10 (Fall 1976): 405-25. Brief but stimulating discussion of Du Bois's "rhetorical excesses. . . . sentence inversions. . . . alliteration," and his use of "pleonastic doublets."

Turner, Darwin. W. E. B. Du Bois and the Theory of a Black Aesthetic." In *Studies in the Literary Imagination* 7 (1975): 1-21. A lucid discussion of Du Bois's significance in developing a black aesthetic, good also for analyzing Du Bois's critical ambivalence.

Walden, Daniel. W. E. B. Du Bois: Pioneer Reconstruction Historian." *Negro History Bulletin* 26 (February 1963): 159-60, 164. Good study of the scholarly background out of which Du Bois produced possibly his greatest work.

Weinberg, Meyer. *W. E. B. Du Bois: A Reader.* New York: Harper & Row, 1970. "Consists entirely of articles by Du Bois that were first published in various magazines." The articles are well selected, the book good for examining the evolution of Du Bois's thought, and for studying how he adapted his materials for book publication. Also contains a helpful introduction and an excellent selected bibliography of works by Du Bois and bibliographies treating him.

WESLEY, CHARLES H. "W. E. B. Du Bois, Historian." *Freedomways* 5 (Winter 1965): 59-72. An excellent resumé of Du Bois's varied skills and attainments as a historian.

————. "Racial Propaganda and Historical Writing," *Opportunity* 13 (August 1935): 244-46, 254. Identifies Du Bois as a "lyric historian." Aptheker, in his essay "W. E. B. Du Bois, The Historian," calls this "the most penetrating review of Du Bois' *Black Reconstruction*."

WILLIAMS, T. HARRY. An Analysis of Some Reconstruction Attitudes." *Journal of Southern History* 12 (November 1946): 469-86. A distinguished historian examines Reconstruction histories. Contains high if qualified critical praise of Du Bois's work.

YELLIN, JEAN. "Du Bois' *Crisis* and Woman's Suffrage." *Massachusetts Review* 14 (Spring 1973): 365-75. Reveals clearly the extent to which Du Bois fought against a wide range of discriminatory practices directed mainly toward black women, but often toward white women as well.

Index